全国英语专业博雅系列教材/总主编　丁建新

博雅阅读·泛读 4

主　编　杨维忠　王清霞
副主编　吕　娅　胡文育　李　彤

·广州·

版权所有　翻印必究

图书在版编目（CIP）数据

博雅阅读·泛读·4/杨维忠，王清霞主编．— 广州：中山大学出版社，2016.2

（全国英语专业博雅系列教材/丁建新总主编）

ISBN 978-7-306-05386-2

Ⅰ.①博… Ⅱ.①杨…②王… Ⅲ.①英语 — 阅读教学 — 高等学校 — 教材　Ⅳ.①H319.4

中国版本图书馆 CIP 数据核字（2015）第 180827 号

出版人：	徐　劲
策划编辑：	熊锡源
责任编辑：	熊锡源
封面设计：	曾　斌
责任校对：	刘学谦
责任技编：	黄少伟
出版发行：	中山大学出版社
电　　话：	编辑部 020-84111996，84113349，84111997，84110779
	发行部 020-84111998，84111981，84111160
地　　址：	广州市新港西路 135 号
邮　　编：	510275　　传　真：020-84036565
网　　址：	http://www.zsup.com.cn　E-mail:zdcbs@mail.sysu.edu.cn
印 刷 者：	广州中大印刷有限公司
规　　格：	787mm×1092mm　1/16　10.5 印张　260 千字
版次印次：	2016 年 2 月第 1 版　2016 年 2 月第 1 次印刷
印　　数：	1～3000 册　　定　价：28.00 元

如发现本书因印装质量影响阅读，请与出版社发行部联系调换

英语专业博雅系列教材编委会

总主编　丁建新（中山大学）

编　委　会

李洪儒（黑龙江大学）
司显柱（北京交通大学）
赵彦春（天津外国语大学）
田海龙（天津外国语大学）
夏慧言（天津科技大学）
李会民（河南科技学院）
刘承宇（西南大学）
施　旭（浙江大学）
辛　斌（南京师范大学）
杨信彰（厦门大学）
徐畅贤（湖南城市学院）
李玉英（江西师范大学）
李发根（江西师范大学）
肖坤学（广州大学）
宫　齐（暨南大学）
张广奎（广东财经大学）
温宾利（广东外语外贸大学）
杜金榜（广东外语外贸大学）
阮　炜（深圳大学）
张晓红（深圳大学）

博雅之辩（代序）

大学精神陷入前所未有的危机，许多人在寻找出路。

我们的坚持是，提倡博雅教育（Liberal Education）。因为大凡提倡什么，关键在于审视问题的症结何在，对症下药。而当下之困局，根源在于功利，在于忘掉了教育之根本。

博雅教育之理念，可以追溯至古罗马人提倡的"七艺"：文法、修辞、辩证法、音乐、算术、几何、天文学。其目的在于培养人格完美的自由思考者。在中国教育史上，博雅的思想，古已有之。中国儒家教育的传统，强调以培养学生人格为核心。儒家"六艺"，礼、乐、射、御、书、数，体现的正是我们所讲的博雅理念。"学识广博，生活高雅"，在这一点上，中国与西方，现代与传统，并无二致。

在古罗马，博雅教育在于培育自由的人格与社会精英。在启蒙时代，博雅教育意指解放思想，破除成见。"什么都知道一点，有些事情知道得多一点"，这是19世纪英国的思想家约翰·斯图亚特·密尔（John Stuart Mill）对博雅的诠释。同一时期，另外一位思想家，曾任都柏林大学校长的约翰·亨利·纽曼（John Henry Newman）在《大学理念》一书中，也曾这样表述博雅的培养目标："如果必须给大学课程一个实际目标，那么，我说它就是训练社会的良好成员。它的艺术是社会生活的艺术，它的目的是对世界的适应……大学训练旨在提高社会的精神格调，培养公众的智慧，纯洁一个民族的趣味"。

博雅教育包括科学与人文，目标在于培养人的自由和理性的精神，而不是迎合市场与风俗。教育的目标在于让学生学会尊重人类生活固有的内在价值：生命的价值、尊严的价值、求知的价值、爱的价值、相互尊重的价值、自我超越的价值、创新的价值。提倡博雅教育，就是要担当这些价值守护者的角色。博雅教育对于我们来说，是一种素质教育、人文教育。人文教育关心人类的终极目标，不是以"有用"为标准。它不是"万金油"，也无关乎"风花雪月"。

在美国，专注于博雅教育的大学称为"文理学院"，拒绝职业性的教育。在中国香港，以博雅教育为宗旨的就有岭南大学，提倡"全人教育"；在台湾大学，博雅教育是大学教育的基础，课程涉及文学与艺术、历史思维、世界文明、道德与哲学、公民意识与社会分析、量化分析与数学素养、物质科学、生命科学等八大领域。在欧洲，博雅教育历史中的七大范畴被分为"三道"（初级）与"四道"（高级）。前者包括语法、修辞与辩证法，后者包括算术、几何、天文与音乐。在中国大陆的中山大学，许多有识之士也提倡博雅之理念，让最好的教授开设通识课程，涉及现代学科之环境、生物、地理等各门。同时设立"博雅学院"，学拉丁，读古典，开风气之先。

外语作为一门人文性很强的学科，尤其有必要落实博雅之理念。对于我们来说，最好的"应用型"教育在于博雅。早在20世纪20～40年代，在水木清华的外文系，吴宓先生提倡"语""文"并重，"中""西"兼修，教学上提倡自主学习与互动研究。在《西洋文学系学程总则》中，吴宓明确了"博雅之士"的培养目标：

> 本系课程编写的目的为使学生：（甲）成为博雅之士；（乙）了解西洋文明之精神；（丙）熟读西方文学之名著、谙悉西方思想之潮流，因而在国内教授英、德、法各国语言文字及文学，足以胜任愉快；（丁）创造今日之中国文学；（戊）汇通东西方之精神而互为介绍传布。

博雅之于我们，不仅仅是理念，更重要的是课程体系，是教材，是教法，是实践，是反应试教育，是将通识与专业熔于一炉。基于这样的理念，我们编写了这套丛书。希望通过这样的教育，让我们的学生知道人之为人是有他内在的生活意义，告诉我们的学生去求知，去阅读，去思考，去创造，去理解世界，去适应社会，去爱，去相互尊重，去审美，去找回精神的家园。

无需辩驳，也不怕非议。这是我们的坚守。

中山大学外国语学院　教授、博士生导师
中山大学语言研究所　所长
丁建新
2013年春天

前　言

《博雅阅读·泛读》是根据《高等学校英语专业基础阶段英语教学大纲》的要求编写的英语专业基础阶段泛读教材，共4册，本书是第4册。教材内容经过严格的筛选和科学的设计，在选材、内容编排、练习设计等方面体现博雅教育理念。本套教材系统、分层次地介绍常见的阅读技巧，指导学生掌握各种阅读方法，快速、准确地获取并处理信息，旨在借助一定的阅读技巧和大量的课文阅读让学生获取广博的知识，循序渐进地提高学生的英语阅读能力。

本教材所选课文内容不求精深，但都高屋建瓴、深入浅出，围绕广义上的博雅教育理念的要求，涉及多门学科，包括文学、法学、教育学、自然科学、天文学、民族学、史学、语言学、经济学、军事学、政治学、伦理学、美学、宗教学、哲学、逻辑学、社会学等，既能反映博雅的理念，又能满足教学的需要。所选文章均出自《华盛顿邮报》《读者》《每日邮报》《每日电讯报》《卫报》等刊物或是英国BBC、美国VOA和CNN等新闻报道。选材保证了内容的权威性、真实性、可读性和实用性，同时避免枯燥、乏味的学术探讨和理论介绍。

《博雅阅读·泛读》第三、四册是对前两册的巩固和提升。经过一年的学习，学生对博雅教育理念及相关学科知识有了初步了解，具备了一定的阅读技巧和思辨能力，因此，第三册和第四册侧重知识性和应用性。《博雅阅读·泛读》第四册共9个单元，分为三个部分，选题分别围绕宗教、美学和演说展开。本册课文选材多出自大家之手，文章立意高远，论证深入，部分课文理解上有一定难度，作为泛读材料，希望能引领学生对问题作出全面、深刻的思考，着力培养学生的批判与思辨能力。练习题目多以问题回答、主旨概括、观点阐述、辩论等形式呈现，强调学生对课文的理解以及观点表达能力，突出开放性、批判性，兼顾实践性。

衷心感谢中山大学出版社对本教材在编写和出版过程中的支持。本教材的部分图片、资料取自互联网，再此一并致谢！

由于编者水平有限，难免有疏漏和谬误之处，欢迎广大专家、学者以及使用本教材的教师、学生等提出意见和批评，以便我们及时改进。

编　者
2015年2月

Contents

Topic 1　Aesthetics ··· 1

  Unit 1　Beauty ·· 2
    Section A: Text-based Reading Comprehension ················· 4
    Section B: Vocabulary ··· 5
    Section C: Cloze ··· 7
    Section D: Reading Skills Training ··································· 8
    Further Reading　What Is Aesthetics ······························· 13
  Unit 2　Beauty and Nature ·· 17
    Section A: Text-based Reading Comprehension ··············· 19
    Section B: Vocabulary ··· 21
    Section C: Cloze ··· 22
    Section D: Reading Skills Training ································· 23
    Further Reading　Yearning for That Piece of Green Meadow ················· 29
  Unit 3　Expecting Beauty ·· 32
    Section A: Text-based Reading Comprehension ··············· 34
    Section B: Vocabulary ··· 35
    Section C: Cloze ··· 36
    Section D: Reading Skills Training ································· 37
    Further Reading　Oscar Wilde: The Philosophy of Beauty ················ 43

Topic 2　Religion ··· 47

  Unit 4　Bound to Be Free ·· 49
    Section A: Text-based Reading Comprehension ··············· 53
    Section B: Vocabulary ··· 55
    Section C: Cloze ··· 56

Section D: Reading Skills Training ······ 57
Further Reading　The Origin of Religion ······ 63

Unit 5　Is the *Bible* True? (Excerpt) ······ 67
Section A: Text-based Reading Comprehension ······ 71
Section B: Vocabulary ······ 72
Section C: Cloze ······ 74
Section D: Reading Skills Training ······ 74
Further Reading　The Da Vinci Code (Excerpt) ······ 79

Unit 6　Religious Art ······ 85
Section A: Text-based Reading Comprehension ······ 88
Section B: Vocabulary ······ 90
Section C: Cloze ······ 91
Section D: Reading Skills Training ······ 92
Further Reading　Religion and Language ······ 97

Topic 3　Speech ······ 103

Unit 7　The Significance of Poetry ······ 104
Section A: Text-based Reading Comprehension ······ 106
Section B: Vocabulary ······ 107
Section C: Cloze ······ 108
Section D: Reading Skills Training ······ 109
Further Reading　The Commencement Address ······ 116

Unit 8　Man's Peril ······ 122
Section A: Text-based Reading Comprehension ······ 126
Section B: Vocabulary ······ 127
Section C: Cloze ······ 128
Section D: Reading Skills Training ······ 129
Further Reading　The Road to Success (Excerpt) ······ 137

Unit 9　Third Inaugural Address ······ 142
Section A: Text-based Reading Comprehension ······ 145
Section B: Vocabulary ······ 147
Section C: Cloze ······ 148
Section D: Reading Skills Training ······ 149
Further Reading　Struggle for Freedom ······ 156

参考文献 ······ 158

Topic 1   Aesthetics

Aesthetics is a branch of philosophy dealing with the nature of art, beauty, and taste, with the creation and appreciation of beauty. It is more scientifically defined as the study of sensory or sensori-emotional values, sometimes called judgments of sentiment and taste. More broadly, scholars in the field define aesthetics as "critical reflection on art, culture and nature."

More specific aesthetic theory, often with practical implications, relating to a particular branch of the arts, is divided into areas of aesthetics such as art theory, literary theory, film theory and music theory.

Selected words on *aesthetics*:

Aestheticism	唯美主义	Art for art's sake	艺术至上主义
Avant-garde	先锋派	Formalism	形式主义
Modernism	现代主义	Naturalism	自然主义
Post-modernism	后现代主义	Post-structuralism	后结构主义
Realism	现实主义	Romanticism	浪漫主义
Symbolism	象征主义	Utopianism	乌托邦主义

Unit 1

Beauty

For the Greeks, beauty was a virtue: a kind of excellence. Persons then were assumed to be what we now have to call — enviously — whole persons. If it did occur to the Greeks to distinguish between a person's "inside" and "outside", they still expected that inner beauty would be matched by beauty of the other kind. The well-born young Athenians who gathered around Socrates found it quite paradoxical that their hero was so intelligent, so brave, so honorable, so seductive — and so ugly. One of Socrates' main pedagogical acts was to be ugly — and teach those innocent, no doubt splendid-looking disciples of his how full of paradoxes life really was.

They may have resisted Socrates' lesson. But we do not. Several thousand years later, we are more wary of the enchantments of beauty. We not only split off — with the greatest facility — the "inside" (character, intellect) from the "outside" (looks); but we are actually surprised when someone who is beautiful is also intelligent, talented, and good.

It was principally the influence of Christianity that deprived beauty of the central place it had in classical ideals of human excellence. By limiting excellence to moral virtue only, Christianity set beauty adrift — as an alienated, arbitrary, superficial enchantment. And beauty has continued to lose prestige. For close to two centuries it has become a convention to attribute beauty to only one of the two sexes: the sex which, however Fair, is always Second. Associating beauty with women has put beauty even further on the defensive, morally.

A beautiful woman, we say in English, but a handsome man. "Handsome" is the masculine equivalent of — and refusal of — a compliment which has accumulated certain demeaning overtones, by being reserved for women only. That one can call a man "beautiful" in French and in Italian suggests that Catholic countries — unlike those countries shaped by the Protestant version of Christianity — still retain some vestiges of the pagan admiration for beauty. But the difference, if one exists, is of degree only. In every modern country that is Christian or post-Christian, women are the beautiful sex — to be detriment of the notion of beauty as well as of women.

To be called beautiful is thought to name something essential to women's character and concerns. (In contrast to men — whose essence is to be strong, or effective, or competent.) It does not take someone in the throes of advanced feminist awareness to perceive that the way women are taught to be involved with beauty encourages narcissism, reinforces dependence and immaturity. Everybody knows that. For it is "everybody", a whole society that has identified being feminine with caring about how one looks. (In contrast to being masculine — which is identified with caring about what one is and does and only secondarily, if at all, about how one looks.) Given these stereotypes, it is no wonder that beauty enjoys, at best, a rather mixed reputation.

It is not, of course, the desire to be beautiful that is wrong but the obligation to be — or to try. What is accepted by most women as a flattering idealization of their sex is a way of making women feel inferior to what they actually are — or normally grow to be. For the ideal of beauty is administered as a form of self-oppression. Women are taught to see their bodies in parts, and to evaluate each part separately. Breasts, feet, hips, waistline, neck, eyes, nose, complexion, hair, and so on — each in turn is submitted to an anxious, fretful, often despairing scrutiny. Even if some pass muster, some will always be found wanting. Nothing less than perfection will do.

In men, good looks is a whole, something taken in at a glance. It does not need to be confirmed by giving measurements of different regions of the body; nobody encourages a man to dissect his appearance, feature by feature. As for perfection, that is considered trivial — almost unmanly. Indeed, in the ideally good-looking man a small imperfection or blemish is considered positively desirable. According to one movie critic (a woman) who is a declared Robert Redford fan, it is having that cluster of skin-colored moles on one cheek that saves Redford from being merely a "pretty face". Think of the depreciation of women — as well as beauty — that is implied in that judgment.

"The privileges of beauty are immense," said Cocteau. To be sure, beauty is a form of power. And deservedly so. What is lamentable is that it is the only form of power that most women are encouraged to seek. This power is always conceived in relation to men; it is not the power to do but the power to attract. It is a power that negates itself. For this power is not one that can be chosen freely — at least, not by women — or renounced without social censure.

To preen, for a woman, can never be just a pleasure. It is also a duty. It is her work. If a woman does real work — and even if she has clambered up to a leading position in politics, law, medicine, business, or whatever — she is always under pressure to confess that she still works at being attractive. But in so far as she is keeping up as one of the Fair Sex, she brings under suspicion her very capacity to be objective, professional, authoritative, and thoughtful. Damned if they do — women are, and damned if they don't.

One could hardly ask for more important evidence of the dangers of considering persons as split between what is "inside" and what is "outside" than that interminable half-comic half-tragic tale, the oppression of women. How easy it is to start off by defining women as caretakers of their surfaces, and then to disparage them or find them adorable for being "superficial". It is a crude trap, and it has worked for too long. But to get out of the trap requires that women get some critical distance from that excellence and privilege which is beauty, enough distance to see how much beauty itself has been abridged in order to prop up the mythology of the "feminine". There should be a way of saving beauty from women — and for them.

(Text source: *Against Interpretation*, by Susan Sontag Picador, 2001.)

Section A: Text-based Reading Comprehension

I. Choose the best answer according to the passage.

1. Why are Greeks' viewpoints on beauty mentioned in paragraph 1?
   A. To illustrate only their paradoxical ideas
   B. To attract readers' attention in referring to history
   C. To draw forth the topic of this passage that shows the difference
   D. To distinguish between a people's "inside" and "outside"
2. Which one of the following is true according to this passage?
   A. For women, to be beautiful is a compulsory desire.
   B. For men, imperfections in body are strongly rejected.
   C. Beauty enjoys an extremely mixed reputation.
   D. It's a duty for women to preen.
3. What profession might the author be?
   A. Feminist writer   B. Columnist
   C. Proser   D. Fictionist
4. Which statement is not in conformity with the author's viewpoint?
   A. Beauty plays a core role in classical ideals of human excellence before Christianity.

B. The essence of beauty to women is different from that to men.
C. Appearance is not important to the beauty of a man.
D. For a woman, to dress herself is not only a pleasure but also a duty.
5. According to the author, the power of beauty _____.
   A. only belong to women
   B. can be a self-negation
   C. can be freely chosen
   D. should be unbiased in gender

II. Answer the following questions.

1. The author claimed in the text that "for close to two centuries it has become a convention to attribute beauty to only one of the two sexes: the sex which, however Fair, is always Second." So, what does "Second" probably mean according to the passage?

   _____
   _____

2. What is "inside" and "outside" beauty according to the author?

   _____
   _____
   _____

III. Further discussion.

1. Cocteau said: "The privileges of beauty are immense." How do you understand it? Then, what's your opinion on beauty and power?

   _____
   _____

2. After studying the passage, what do you think women should do to realize their value and potential and to avoid the "crude trap" mentioned by the author?

   _____
   _____
   _____

Section B: Vocabulary

I. Fill in the blanks with the proper forms of the words given below.

seductive	facility	deprive	adrift	detriment
reinforce	dissect	conceive	negate	interminable
disparage	scrutiny	censure	clamber	fretful

1. He works long hours, to the _____ of his health.

2. Matcham's theatres were widely _____ by architects.
3. This offer of a high salary and a free house is very _____.
4. Careful _____ of the company's accounts revealed a whole series of errors.
5. UNHCR reports at least 52 Somalis died when the boat smuggling them across the Gulf of Aden to Yemen broke down, leaving them _____ with no food or water for 18 days.
6. Your assignment is to _____ the poem.
7. In fact, it has no choice: if history, by unfolding unpredictably, were allowed to demonstrate that ideology is wrong, it would _____ power of its legitimacy.
8. If we _____ the traffic security education and more people comply with traffic regulations, I believe one day traffic accidents can be avoided.
9. Today, the sound of cascading market crashes seems to be drowning both the _____ and the exuberant China-India chatter — but not completely, probably not for long, and not equally in all places.
10. It is likely that an Italian with a working _____ in English would have been hired, but my friend did not look Italian.
11. Seemingly _____, the light-hearted frolics of the first movie feel like an eternity ago.
12. I cannot _____ why you allowed the child to go alone.
13. When Erskine asked Newt why they would proceed with impeachment instead of other possible remedies such as _____ or reprimand, the Speaker replied, because we can.
14. For all its promise, the new continental perspective does not _____ the maritime one, and sometimes reinforces it.
15. Following a muddy track, in which a few diminutive nun-sized shoe-prints have survived the rain, I cross a foaming torrent, then _____ up the other side.

II. Root and word formation.
A. Study the following roots and list more examples in the space provided.

Root	Meaning	Examples	More examples
-scend	to climb	ascend, transcend	
-sci	to know	prescience, conscious	
-scrib	to write	ascribe, transcribe	
-serv	to serve, to keep	conserve, deserve, preserve	
-sign	sign, mark	consign, assign, resign	

B. Fill in the blanks with the proper forms of the words given below.

transcribe	conserve	conscious	ascend
reserve	transcend	prescience	prescribe

1. He hurt his head in the accident, but he is still _____.
2. We must _____ our forests if we are to make sure of a future supply of wood.
3. The stairs _____ in a graceful curve.
4. The doctor _____ some tranquilizers and a few days of rest.
5. All rights _____.
6. Thanks to his _____, he got out of the stock market before it fell.
7. I record my professor's lectures and _____ them at home.
8. She far _____ the others in beauty and intelligence.

Section C: Cloze

Direction: Fill in the blanks with the proper forms of the words given below.

| without | that | remind | unusual | because |
| experiment | cause | whatever | consume | exercise |

Drinking eight cups or two liters of water a day is longstanding advice. But is there any scientific basis for it, asks Dr Chris van Tulleken. You know those ads that __1__ us that even a small drop in hydration levels can massively affect performance so you need to keep hydrated with __2__ brand of isotonic super drink they're selling? They seem pretty scientific, don't they? Man in white coat, athlete with electrodes attached and so on. And it's not a hard sell __3__ drinking feels right — you're hot and sweating so surely replacing __4__ fluid must be beneficial. Well earlier this year, sports scientists in Australia did an extraordinary __5__ that had never been done before. This group wanted to find out what happened to performance after dehydration. So they took a group of cyclists and __6__ them until they lost 3% of their total body weight in sweat. Then their performance was assessed after rehydration with either 1) nothing, 2) enough water to bring them back to 2% dehydration or 3) after full rehydration. So far nothing __7__, but the difference between this and almost every other study that's ever been done on hydration was that the cyclists were blind to how much water they got. The fluid was given intravenously __8__ them knowing the volume. This is vital because we all, and especially athletes, have such an intimate psychological relationship with water __9__.

Remarkably, there was no performance difference between those that were fully rehydrated and those that got nothing. This study was part of a growing movement to "drink to thirst" which hopes to persuade athletes not to over-hydrate with the potentially fatal consequence of diluting your sodium level, __10__ hyponatraemia. Perhaps the result shouldn't be so surprising. Humans evolved doing intense exercise in extreme heat and dryness.

8 博雅阅读·泛读 4

Section D: Reading Skills Training

Directions: The following exercises are meant to improve your fast reading ability. And you are suggested to go over the passages quickly and then answer all the questions within 25 minutes.

Passage 1
For questions 1 –7, please mark
    Y (for YES) if the statement agrees with the information given in the passage;
    N (for NO) if the statement contradicts the information given in the passage;
    NG (for NOT GIVEN) if the statement is not given in the passage.

For questions 8 –10, complete the sentences with the information given in the passage.

1. _____ The outcome of the Labor pilot scheme to provide free school meals for every primary pupil is impressive but local council has decided to withdraw Government cash.
2. _____ Besides dealing with obesity and improving children's health and eating habits, the scheme also intends to help improve their behavior and academic performance.
3. _____ Up to 75% of St Winefride's children are now taking part in the scheme.
4. _____ According to Paul Underwood, the performance of children on free school meals was better than that of many of the others.
5. _____ School Food Report in 2010 requires that the school lunch program should be carried out all over UK.
6. _____ The council's cabinet member for children and young people, Quintin Peppiatt, says that the scheme may not lessen the burden of health services.
7. _____ The most important thing for the meal is that they are tasty and nutritional.
8. According to Mr Peppiatt, universal free school meals are more cost-efficient for schools due to _____.
9. All the children on St Winefride's pupil council have at least one parent working in the evenings, so a home-cooked meal is _____.
10. Based on the School Food Trust, the school lunch should provide children with _____.

Mind over Platter

    A Labour pilot scheme to provide free school meals for every primary pupil is achieving such impressive results that the local council has pledged to fund it once Government cash is withdrawn.

It is lunchtime at St Winefride's Roman Catholic Primary and the dinner hall is heaving. The queue for food is bustling and in constant flux as eager youngsters run to the front to eye up today's offering and try to jump ahead.

Roast lamb seems to be the most popular choice today, along with the sweetcorn, but no matter what's on their plate, every tray has a piece of melon or a selection of summer berries. The doors open on to the playground, where younger pupils have had their fill and are playing with hula hoops, competing to see who can keep theirs spinning the longest.

St Winefride's is in the borough of Newham, east London, one of three local authorities in the country taking part in a Government-funded pilot scheme to provide free school meals for every primary pupil, not just those who qualify on income grounds. As well as tackling obesity and improving children's health and eating habits, the scheme also aims to bring benefits in behaviour and academic performance.

The take-up at St Winefride's has been dramatic. Almost all — 98 percent — of its 300 pupils are opting for a hot meal at lunchtime, compared with 27 percent previously. This has been mirrored across the rest of the borough, where up to 75 percent of children are taking part.

As areas of high deprivation where the intended impact could be felt most, Newham, Durham and Wolverhampton were chosen to participate in the pilot. Newham has the second-highest obesity rate in the country for Year 6 pupils and the third highest for reception children.

On top of this, 52 percent of children in the borough experience childhood poverty, defined as less than 60 percent of the median UK household income, which is currently £ 407 per week.

Munachim, a self-confessed junk-food lover, now eats lunch at school every day. "Before, I would eat cake, chocolate, and sometimes take away chips for lunch. I didn't eat my sandwiches, and I'd be asking my parents for unhealthy food," he says. Now he enjoys cooked lunches and has more energy during the school day. "My dad thinks it is really good, too — he saves lots of money," adds the 11-year-old.

The impact of the pilot programme is being monitored over two years, but Paul Underwood, headteacher at St Winefride's, is already convinced of its value.

"I was always surprised at our school because the children on free school meals did better than many of the others," he says. "It is supposed to be the other way around, but the children who brought in packed lunches didn't do so well, academically and in terms of behaviour."

The previous Labour government had planned to widen free school meals provision to a further 500,000 children from this September, and to extend the pilot scheme to another five local authorities: Bradford, Nottingham, Cumbria, Medway in Kent and the London borough of Islington. But Education Secretary Michael Gove shelved both plans earlier this year on cost grounds, although the existing pilots were allowed to continue until their original end date next July.

At St Winefride's, the number of pupils eligible for free school meals was lower than in many other Newham schools — 10 percent, compared with a borough average of 50 percent. But making the meals free for all has had a noticeable effect in the classroom, says Mr Underwood.

"We can teach English and maths in the afternoon now, as the children can actually concentrate after lunch," he says. "They feel better in themselves, and you can tell."

Since a nutritional standard was introduced by the School Food Trust in 2008, a school lunch is required to provide children with essential vitamins and nutrients. Packed lunches, by contrast, are more likely to be filled with junk food.

The impact of healthy food has been so great that the school has set up a breakfast club at a daily cost of £ 1 for every pupil.

For the past few years, the school provided breakfast for Year 6 pupils during the week of their Sats exams to make sure they had a good start to the day and were calm and settled in the morning.

Sometimes Victoria, 11, does not have time to make breakfast for herself. Her mother works long hours and it is usually her sister who cooks dinner. "Before we got free school meals, I made (lunch) myself, but I'd usually have chocolate," she says with a cheeky grin. During Sats week, when she was having breakfast and lunch at school, Victoria's mother noticed that her daughter was more alert and less irritable.

While most families of pupils at St Winefride's would not qualify for free school meals under the previous system, many are in low-income jobs and the cost of paying for a school dinner could be a significant disincentive.

"They're very caring parents, but a busy lifestyle means they don't have enough time to prepare healthy meals," says Mr Underwood. "Lots of them are nurses or cleaners. They might have to be at work at half seven in the morning."

Although Government funding for the scheme will finish at the end of this academic year, the local authority has been so impressed by the results so far that it has pledged to keep it going. As well as matching the £ 2 million from central government, the authority has also found £ 1.6 million to cope with the higher-than-expected demand for school meals.

The council's cabinet member for children and young people, Quintin Peppiatt, says he is convinced that the scheme will end up paying for itself. "The levels of obesity and malnutrition are in the top ten for the country," he says. "Some of the problems in the home are linked to poor health, and providing universal free school meals should help with that, putting less pressure on the health services."

Universal free school meals are also more cost-efficient for schools, coming out 10 percent cheaper to run than the previous system due to reduced administration costs, according to Mr Peppiatt. "It has also put 180 local people into work and they have the opportunity to train and get further qualifications," he says.

Providing primary children with free school meals does not change children's attitudes to food overnight, if the 10-strong pupil council at St Winefride's is anything to go by — all of the children, aged from six to 11, admit to eating and loving take-away chicken and chips several times a week.

All the children on St Winefride's pupil council have at least one parent who works in the evenings, so a home-cooked meal is a special occasion.

"When my mum is not well, we have sausages," says eight-year-old Rajeevi. "But if my mum is well, we have curry and rice."

But as far as these pupil representatives are concerned, the free school meals pilot is a success. "Everyone's looking forward to lunch now," says Munachim.

For Rajeevi, the most important thing is not that the meals are tasty or that they meet a nutritional standard, but that they are there. "I love having school meals," she says. "Afterwards, I feel full."

Passage 2

In our discussion of instincts we saw that there was reason to believe that whatever we inherit must be of some very simple sort rather than any complicated or very definite kind of behavior. It is certain that no one inherits knowledge of mathematics. It may be, however, that children inherit more or less of a rather general ability that we may call intelligence. If very intelligent children become deeply interested in mathematics, they will probably make a success of that study.

As for musical ability, it may be that what is inherited is an especially sensitive ear, a peculiar structure of the hands or the vocal organs connections between nerves and muscles that make it comparatively easy to learn the movements a musician must execute, and particularly vigorous emotions. If these factors are all organized around music, the child may become a musician. The same factors, in other circumstance might be organized about some other center of interest. The rich emotional equipment might find expression in poetry. The capable fingers might develop skill in surgery. It is not the knowledge of music that is inherited, then nor even the love of it, but a certain bodily structure that makes it comparatively easy to acquire musical knowledge and skill. Whether that ability shall be directed toward music or some other undertaking may be decided entirely by forces in the environment in which a child grows up.

Read the passage above and answer the following questions.

11. It is possible that children inherit a general ability rather than specific knowledge. _____ (Y/N/NG)
12. Children's ability to music is decided entirely by the environment where they grow up. _____ (Y/N/NG)
13. What children inherit about music is _____.

Passage 3

Racket, din clamor, noise, hatever you want to call it, unwanted sound is America's most widespread nuisance. But noise is more than just a nuisance. It constitutes a real and present danger to people's health. Day and night, at home, at work, and at play, noise can produce serious physical and psychological stress. No one is immune to this stress. Though we seem to adjust to noise by ignoring it, the ear, in fact, never closes and the body still responds — sometimes with extreme tension, as to a strange sound in the night.

The annoyance we feel when faced with noise is the most common outward symptom of the stress building up inside us. Indeed, because irritability is so apparent, legislators have made public annoyance the basis of many noise abatement programs. The more subtle and more serious health hazards associated with stress caused by noise traditionally have been given much less attention. Nevertheless, when we are annoyed or made irritable by noise, we should consider these symptoms fair warning that other thing may be happening to us, some of which may be damaging to our health.

Of many health hazards to noise, hearing loss is the most clearly observable and measurable by health professionals. The other hazards are harder to pin down. For many of us, there may be a risk that exposure to the stress of noise increases susceptibility to disease and infection. The more susceptible among us may experience noise as a complicating factor in heart problems and other diseases. Noise that causes annoyance and irritability in health persons may have serious consequences for these already ill in mind or body.

Read the passage above and answer the following questions.
14. Our stress caused by noise has been given much attention. _____ (Y/N/NG)
15. For health professionals, hearing loss is the most _____.

Further Reading

What Is Aesthetics

The full field of what might be called "Aesthetics" is a very large one. There is even now a four-volume encyclopedia devoted to the full range of possible topics. The core issues in Philosophical Aesthetics, however, are nowadays fairly settled.

Aesthetics in this central sense has been said to start in the early eighteenth century, with the series of articles on "The Pleasures of the Imagination" which the journalist Joseph Addison wrote in the early issues of the magazine *The Spectator* in 1712. Before this time, thoughts by notable figures made some forays into this ground, for instance in the formulation of general theories of proportion and harmony, detailed most specifically in Architecture and Music. But the full development of extended, philosophical reflection on Aesthetics did not begin to emerge until the widening of leisure activities in the eighteenth century.

SELECTIONS FROM THE WRITINGS OF JOSEPH ADDISON

By far the most thoroughgoing and influential of the early theorists was Immanuel Kant, towards the end of the eighteenth century. Therefore it is important, first of all, to have some sense of how Kant approached the subject. Through him, we can meet some of the key concepts in the subject by way of introduction.

Kant is sometimes thought of as a formalist in Art Theory; that is to say, someone who thinks the content of a work of art is not of aesthetic interest. But this is only part of the story. Certainly he was a formalist about the pure enjoyment of Nature, but for Kant most of the arts were impure, because they involved a "concept." Even the enjoyment of parts of Nature was impure, namely when a concept was involved — as when we admire the perfection of an animal body or a human torso. But our enjoyment of, for instance, the arbitrary abstract patterns in some foliage, or a color field (as with wild poppies, or a sunset) was, according to Kant, absent of such concepts; in such cases, the cognitive powers were in free play. By design, Art may sometimes obtain the appearance of this freedom: it was then "Fine Art" — but for Kant not all Art had this quality.

In all, Kant's theory of pure beauty had four aspects: its freedom from concepts, its objectivity, the disinterest of the spectator, and its obligatoriness. By "concept,"

Kant meant "end," or "purpose," i. e., what the cognitive powers of human understanding and imagination judge applies to an object, such as with "it is a pebble," to take an instance. But when no definite concept is involved, as with the scattered pebbles on a beach, the cognitive powers are held to be in free play; and it is when this play is harmonious that there is the experience of pure beauty. There is also objectivity and universality in  the judgment then, according to Kant, since the cognitive powers are common to all who can judge that the individual objects are pebbles. These powers function alike whether they come to such a definite judgment or are left suspended in free play, as when appreciating the pattern along the shoreline. This was not the basis on which the apprehension of pure beauty was obligatory, however. According to Kant, that which was derived from the selflessness of such an apprehension was called in the eighteenth century "disinterest." This arises because pure beauty does not gratify us sensuously; nor does it induce any desire to possess the object. It "pleases," certainly, but in a distinctive intellectual way. Pure beauty, in other words, simply holds our mind's attention: we have no further concern than contemplating the object itself. Perceiving the object in such cases is an end in itself; it is not a means to a further end, and is enjoyed for its own sake alone.

It is because Morality requires we rise above ourselves that such an exercise in selfless attention becomes obligatory. Judgments of pure beauty, being selfless, initiate one into the moral point of view. "Beauty is a symbol of Morality," and "The enjoyment of nature is the mark of a good soul" are key sayings of Kant. The shared enjoyment of a sunset or a beach shows there is harmony between us all, and the world.

Among these ideas, the notion of "disinterest" has had much the widest currency. Indeed, Kant took it from eighteenth century theorists before him, such as the moral philosopher, Lord Shaftesbury, and it has attracted much attention since: recently by the French sociologist Pierre Bourdieu, for instance. Clearly, in this context "disinterested" does not mean "uninterested," and paradoxically it is closest to what we now call our "interests," i. e., such things as Hobbies, Travel, and Sport, as we shall see below. But in earlier centuries, one's "interest" was what was to one's advantage, i. e., it was "self-interest," and so it was the negation of that which closely related Aesthetics to Ethics.

The eighteenth century was a surprisingly peaceful time, but this turned out to be the lull before the storm, since out of its orderly classicism there developed a wild romanticism in Art and Literature, and even revolution in politics. The aesthetic concept which came to be more appreciated in this period was associated with this, namely Sublimity, which Edmund Burke theorized about in his "A Philosophical Enquiry into the Origin of our ideas of the Sublime and Beautiful." The Sublime was connected more with pain than pure pleasure, according to Burke, since threats to self-preservation were involved, as on the high seas, and lonely moors, with the devilish humans and dramatic passions that artists and writers were about to portray. But in these circumstances, of course, it is still "delightful horror," as Burke appreciated, since one is insulated by the fictionality of the work in question from any real danger.

"Sublime" and "beautiful" are only two amongst the many terms which may be used to describe our aesthetic experiences. Clearly there are "ridiculous" and "ugly," for a start, as well. But the more discriminating will have no difficulty also finding something maybe "fine," or "lovely" rather than "awful" or "hideous," and "exquisite" or "superb" rather than "gross" or "foul." Frank Sibley wrote a notable series of articles, starting in 1959, defending a view of aesthetic concepts as a whole. He said that they were not rule or condition governed, but required a heightened form of perception, which one might call Taste, Sensitivity, or Judgment. His full analysis, however, contained another aspect, since he was not only concerned with the sorts of concepts mentioned above, but also with a set of others which had a rather different character. For one can describe works of art, often enough, in terms of which relate primarily to the emotional and mental life of human beings. One can call them "joyful," "melancholy," "serene," "witty," "vulgar," and "humble," for instance. These are evidently not purely aesthetic terms, because of their further uses, but they are still very relevant to many aesthetic experiences.

Sibley's claim about these concepts was that there were no sufficient conditions for their application. For many concepts — sometimes called "closed" concepts, as a result — both necessary and sufficient conditions for their application can be given. To be a bachelor, for instance, it is necessary to be male and unmarried, though of marriageable age, and together these three conditions are sufficient. For other concepts, however, the so-called "open" ones, no such definitions can be given — although for aesthetic concepts Sibley pointed out there were still some necessary conditions, since certain facts can rule out the application of, for example, "garish," "gaudy," or "flamboyant."

I. Read the passage above and decide whether the statement is true (T) or false (F).

_____ 1. As a formalist, Kant paid little attention to the content of a work of art.

_____ 2. "Disinterest" means that an object just attracts us and makes us enjoyed for its own sake.

_____ 3. When we mention about the scattered pebbles on a beach we saw in a journey, we actually talk about pure beauty.

_____ 4. Frank Sibley's work only concerned with the concepts of Taste, Sensitivity and Judgment.

_____ 5. Our enjoyment of the arbitrary abstract patterns in foliage was absent of aesthetic concepts according to Kant.

_____ 6. The pure beauty of an object will let us have the desire to possess the object.

_____ 7. "Aesthetics" originated from Joseph Addison's "The pleasures of the Imagination" in 1721.

_____ 8. According to the text, "vulgar" and "humble" are not aesthetic terms, but they are relevant to aesthetic experience.

II. Research & mini-presentation:

To what extent do you agree that <u>beauty is pure</u>? Do some researches in the library or on the internet, and then present your idea to the class.

_____
_____
_____

Unit 2

Beauty and Nature

Judging from the scientists I know, including Eva and Ruth, and those whom I've read about, you can't pursue the laws of nature very long without bumping into beauty. "I don't know if it's the same beauty you see in the sunset," a friend tells me, "but it feels the same." This friend is a physicist, who has spent a long career deciphering what must be happening in the interior of stars. He recalls for me this thrill on grasping for the first time Dirac's equations describing quantum mechanics, or those of Einstein describing relativity. "They're so beautiful," he says, "you can see immediately they have to be true. Or at least on the way toward truth." I ask him what makes a theory beautiful, and he replies, "Simplicity, symmetry, elegance, and power."

Why nature should conform to theories we find beautiful is far from obvious. The most incomprehensible thing about the universe, as Einstein said, is that it's comprehensible. How unlikely, that a short-lived biped on a two-bit planet should be able to gauge the speed of light, lay bare the structure of an atom, or calculate the gravitational tug of a black hole. We're a long way from understanding everything, but we do understand a great deal about how nature behaves. Generation after generation, we puzzle out formulas, test them, and find, to an astonishing degree, that nature agrees. An architect draws designs on flimsy paper, and her buildings stand up through earthquakes.

We launch a satellite into orbit and use it to bounce messages from continent to continent. The machine on which I write these words embodies hundreds of insights into the workings of the material world, insights that are confirmed by every burst of letters on the screen, and I stare at that screen through lenses that obey the laws of optics first worked out in detail by Isaac Newton.

By discerning patterns in the universe, Newton believed, he was tracing the hand of God. Scientists in our day have largely abandoned the notion of a Creator as an unnecessary hypothesis, or at least an untestable one. While they share Newton's faith that the universe is ruled everywhere by a coherent set of rules, they cannot say, as scientists, how these particular rules came to govern things. You can do science without believing in a divine Legislator, but not without believing in laws.

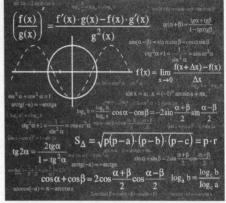

I spent my teenage years scrambling up the mountain of mathematics. Midway up the slope, however, I staggered to a halt, gasping in the rarefied air, well before I reached the heights where the equations of Einstein and Dirac would have made sense. Nowadays I add, subtract, multiply, and do long division when no calculator is handy, and I can do algebra and geometry and even trigonometry in a pinch, but that is about all that I've kept from the language of numbers. Still, I remember glimpsing patterns in mathematics that seemed as bold and beautiful as a skyful of stars.

I'm never more aware of the limitations of language than when I try to describe beauty. Language can create its own loveliness, of course, but it cannot deliver to us the radiance we apprehend in the world, any more than a photograph can capture the stunning swiftness of a hawk or the withering power of a supernova. Eva's wedding album holds only a faint glimmer of the wedding itself. All that pictures or words can do is gesture beyond themselves toward the fleeting glory that stirs our hearts. So I keep gesturing.

"All nature is meant to make us think of paradise," Thomas Merton observed. Because the Creation puts on a nonstop show, beauty is free and inexhaustible, but we need training in order to perceive more than the most obvious kinds. Even 15 billion years or so after the Big Bang, echoes of that event still linger in the form of background radiation, only a few degrees above absolute zero.

Just so, I believe, the experience of beauty is an echo of the order and power that permeate the universe. To measure background radiation, we need subtle instruments; to measure beauty, we need alert intelligence and our five keen senses.

Anyone with eyes can take delight in a face or a flower. You need training, however, to perceive the beauty in mathematics or physics or chess, in the architecture of a tree, the design of a bird's wing, or the shiver of breath through a flute. For most of human history, the training has come from elders who taught the young how to pay attention. By paying attention, we learn to savor all sorts of patterns, from quantum mechanics to patchwork quilts. This predilection brings with it a clear evolutionary advantage, for the ability to recognize patterns helped our ancestors to select mates, find food, and avoid predators. But the same advantage would apply to all species, and yet we alone compose symphonies and crossword puzzles, carve stone into statues, map time and space.

Have we merely carried our animal need for shrewd perceptions to an absurd extreme? Or have we stumbled onto a deep congruence between the structure of our minds and the structure of the universe?

I am persuaded the latter is true. I am convinced there's more to beauty than biology, more than cultural convention. It flows around and through us in such abundance, and in such myriad forms, as to exceed by a wide margin any mere evolutionary need. Which is not to say that beauty has nothing to do with survival: I think it has everything to do with survival. Beauty feeds us from the same source that created us.

It reminds us of the shaping power that reaches through the flower stem and through our own hands. It restores our faith in the generosity of nature. By giving us a taste of the kinship between our own small minds and the great Mind of the Cosmos, beauty reassures us that we are exactly and wonderfully made for life on this glorious planet, in this magnificent universe. I find in that affinity a profound source of meaning and hope. A universe so prodigal of beauty may actually need us to notice and respond, may need our sharp eyes and brimming hearts and teeming minds, in order to close the circuit of Creation.

(Text source: *Hunting for Hope*, by Scott Russell Sanders, 1999.)

Section A: Text-based Reading Comprehension

I. Choose the best answer according to the passage.
1. What is comprehensible about the universe according to the author?
   A. Why nature should conform to theories we find beautiful.
   B. Why the universe is comprehensible.
   C. How nature behaves.
   D. How people on earth should lay bare the structure of an atom.
2. What cannot make a theory beautiful according to this passage?
   A. Prediction   B. Simplicity   C. Power   D. Symmetry
3. Which way of finding beauty doesn't need training?
   A. To practice the beauty in mathematics

B. To find beauty in the shiver of breathe through a flute
   C. To appreciate more beauty than the most obvious kinds
   D. To recognize beauty in tulip
4. Which statement below is true based on this passage?
   A. Beauty feeds us from a different source where we are made.
   B. Beauty is interrelated with survival.
   C. Beauty restores our faith in the generosity of the universe.
   D. Beauty can be easily perceived in our life.
5. Which of the following statements is false?
   A. The author was a student studying mathematics.
   B. People who do science must believe in Divine Legislators.
   C. Our universe is permeated by order and power.
   D. Beauty has something to do with our survival.

II. Answer the following questions.

1. What does the sentence mean by Thomas Merton: "All nature is meant to make us think of paradise"?

   _____
   _____

2. What kind of beauty does the author mainly discuss in this passage?

   _____
   _____

III. Further discussion.

1. In the passage, a friend of the author said: "I don't know if it's the same beauty you see in the sunset, but it feels the same." What is your opinion about it?

   _____
   _____

2. As is stated in the end of the text, beauty needs our sharp eyes, brimming hearts and teeming minds to notice and respond. So, what is beauty in your eyes?

   _____
   _____

Unit 2 Beauty and Nature

Section B: Vocabulary

I. Fill in the blanks with the proper forms of the words given below.

decipher	gauge	conform	embody	discern
abandon	stagger	rarefied	radiance	stunning
permeate	predilection	congruence	prodigal	restore

1. Rescuers had _____ all hope of finding any more survivors.
2. I always wonder how people manage to _____ my doctor's handwriting.
3. Sometimes, the rules may not be _____ with the requirements of the law.
4. The audience was awed into silence by her _____ performance.
5. He picked up the heavy suitcase and set off with a(n) _____.
6. It is often difficult to _____ the truth of an event from a newspaper report.
7. He looked at me, trying to _____ my reaction.
8. The table has a plastic coating which prevents liquids from _____ into the wood beneath.
9. Everyone ought to _____ his spiritual life.
10. Any incomes policy must _____ the attributes of fairness and flexibility.
11. At night these streets are brilliant with a pearly _____ of electricity.
12. There have been rumours that he has been _____ with company funds.
13. Many of us _____ to the outdated customs laid down by our forebears.
14. Ever since she was a child, she has had a _____ for spicy food.
15. The government is trying to _____ public confidence in its management of the economy.

II. Root and word formation.

A. Study the following roots and list more examples in the space provided.

Root	Meaning	Examples	More examples
-solv (solu)	to loosen, to free	absolve, dissolve, resolution	
-spect (spec)	to look, to see	aspect, inspect	
-spir	to breath	aspire, conspire, expire	
-stinct	to brick, to bind	instinct, distinct	

B. Fill in the blanks with the proper forms of the words given below.

dissolve	expect	instinct	aspire
resolution	inspire	distinct	inspect

1. At the meeting, there was a(n) _____ for building a new library.
2. He _____ to the leadership of the party.

3. We _____ to make a small profit this year.
4. Those two ideas are quite _____ from each other.
5. Sugar _____ in water.
6. His best music was _____ by the memory of his mother.
7. Trust your _____ and do what you think is right.
8. After the crash both drivers got out and _____ their cars for damage.

Section C: Cloze

Fill in the blanks with the proper forms of the words given below.

| behold | therefore | which | past | show |
| between | example | earlier | up | circumstance |

He went up the steps, feeling that he was a blighted being. The glass door was opened for him; the servants were as solemn as jackasses under the curry comb. So far, Eugene had only been in the ballroom on the ground floor of the Hotel Beauseant; the fete had followed so closely on the invitation, that he had not had time to call on his cousin, and had __1__ never seen Mme. de Beauseant's apartments; he was about to __2__ for the first time a great lady among the wonderful and elegant surroundings that reveal her character and reflect her daily life. He was the more curious, because Mme. de Restaud's drawing-room had provided him with a standard of comparison.

At half-past four the Vicomtesse de Beauseant was visible. Five minutes __3__ she would not have received her cousin, but Eugene knew nothing of the recognized routine of various houses in Paris. He was conducted __4__ the wide, white-painted, crimson carpeted staircase, __5__ the gilded balusters and masses of flowering plants, to Mme. de Beauseant's apartments. He did not know the rumor current about Mme. de Beauseant, one of the biographies told, with variations, in whispers, every evening in the salons of Paris.

For three years __6__ her name had been spoken of in connection with that of one of the wealthiest and distinguished Portuguese nobles, the Marquis d'Ajuda-Pinto. It was one of those innocent liaisons __7__ possess so much charm for the two thus attached to each other that they find the presence of a third person intolerable. The Vicomte de Beauseant, therefore, had himself set an __8__ to the rest of the world by respecting, with as good a grace as might be, this morganatic union. Any one who came to call on the Vicomtesse in the early days of this friendship was sure to find the Marquis d'Ajuda-Pinto there. As, under the __9__, Mme. de Beauseant could not very well shut her door against these visitors, she gave them such a cold reception, and __10__ so much interest in the study of the ceiling, that no one could fail to understand how much he bored her; and when it became known in Paris that Mme. de Beauseant was bored by callers between two and four o'clock, she was left in perfect solitude during that interval.

Section D: Reading Skills Training

Directions: The following exercises are meant to improve your fast reading ability. And you are suggested to go over the passages quickly and then answer all the questions within 25 minutes.

Passage 1
For questions 1 – 7, please mark
    Y (for YES) if the statement agrees with the information given in the passage;
    N (for NO) if the statement contradicts the information given in the passage;
    NG (for NOT GIVEN) if the statement is not given in the passage.

For questions 8 – 10, complete the sentences with the information given in the passage.

1. _____ Adrian Swain was fired from St Paul's Way Community School for being not willing to follow an official dress code.
2. _____ According to the University and College Union (UCU), the lecturers of Birmingham Metropolitan College acted like "fashion police".
3. _____ A Conservative government announced that it would reward the teacher who looked smart in the classroom.
4. _____ To some teachers, dress code is just one unwelcome intrusion into their professional judgment.
5. _____ According to Mr Haigh, if teachers are expected to suited and booted, they should receive some kind of allowance to buy suits and boots.
6. _____ A handful of surveys suggest that smart teachers fare better.
7. _____ Rosie Cairns completely believed that what teacher wore was of great importance.
8. According to Ms Cairns, _____ can determine how receptive pupils are to teachers.
9. To Mr Varney, asking staff to dress smartly is to _____ between the teacher and the learner.
10. Ms Smith is _____ about how you dress at work.

"If I wanted to wear a suit, I would have worked in a bank"

    Being told you "dress like a teacher" has never been the pinnacle of praise. For many, it conjures up an image of Bill "Scruffy" McGuffy, the Grange Hill teacher Mrs McClusky was always trying to smarten up.

But an increasing number of schools are now demanding that staff revamp their image. Dress codes have become so strict in some places that teachers who defy them may even be sent home to change.

Adrian Swain didn't get that option. The maths and science teacher was fired from St Paul's Way Community School in Tower Hamlets in December for refusing to follow an unofficial dress code. Instead, he continued to turn up to work in trainers and tracksuit bottoms — just as he had for the past 17 years. He has since lost an appeal against the sacking.

And last month the University and College Union (UCU) led a protest against Birmingham Metropolitan College after lecturers were told they would be sent home if they failed to comply with the new dress code: staff were told to wear a business suit or smart skirt and blouse, plus keep their hair "neat, tidy and well groomed". The union accused the college of acting like the "fashion police".

But if there is a change of government, dress codes could even enter the policy agenda. Michael Gove, shadow schools secretary, has already announced that a Conservative government would back schools that introduce smart dress codes for staff, saying that it helps boost the "professional standing" of teachers.

But is it really so important to look smart in the classroom? Only if it improves attainment, insists Mr Swain. The rest is simply window dressing; at worst, masking more serious problems, such as poor leadership.

"What raises standards is good teaching and learning, not what staff wear," agrees Nick Varney, the UCU official for the West Midlands, which represents Birmingham Metropolitan College. Nothing agitates staff more than a dress code, he adds, especially one that is imposed without consultation.

"I have no problem with staff who choose to wear a suit, but if you force everyone to power-dress in order to create an environment of professionalism, it shows there are issues there."

College students, who don't wear uniforms, may enjoy the fact that their lecturers don't look like teachers, Mr Varney adds.

But most primary and secondary pupils do have a uniform. And if they are wearing a jacket and tie, shouldn't their teachers follow suit?

All eight of the academies run by the Ark education charity have imposed strict pupil uniforms. And, on a more informal basis, staff are expected to look smart, too. That means a suit, collar and tie for men and "the equivalent" for women. The new Walworth Academy in south London is the only Ark school to make its rules compulsory. Devon Hanson, the principal, has asked his staff not to wear denim or leather into work.

"It's mostly self-regulating," says Lesley Smith from Ark schools, who insists that the vast majority of academy staff agree with the dress code.

"We want pupils to take pride in their school and themselves and we expect teachers to model that in their appearance. The staff dress code is not as prescriptive as the rules for pupils, but we will take individuals to one side if they look dishevelled or untidy."

However, not all teachers are comfortable with being told what to wear. To them, it is just one more unwelcome intrusion into their professional judgment.

One primary school teacher insists she dresses appropriately for her job, which may include sitting on the floor, messing around with paint and joining in with football in the playground. "If I wanted to wear a suit, I would have worked in a bank," she says.

Another teacher, who does wear a suit in keeping with her school's policy, resented being "told off" for allowing the back of her shirt to become untucked under her jacket. "They treat us like children," she says.

But where should schools draw the line? Few would disagree that short skirts, revealing tops and stiletto heels are neither appropriate nor practical for working in a classroom.

"A couple of my teaching assistants either look like ladies of the night or as if they are in weekend denim mode. I feel for our very devout Muslim parents," says one anonymous primary school headteacher, who directs staff to the school's handbook, which outlines house rules regarding dress. "I don't want to create a staff of Stepford Wives or husbands but it helps to have something concrete written down which can back me up."

A lot of heads impose a dress code because they can't bring themselves to tackle people individually, believes Gerald Haigh, a former primary school headteacher. "The blanket dress code can become a big stick that's really directed at just one or two people," he says.

That is certainly the case for one headteacher. He asks staff to dress "professionally and appropriately" via the school handbook, after a female member of staff kept turning up to school in micro-skirts and fishnet stockings.

Mr Haigh remembers working for a head in the Seventies who instructed a male teacher to wear narrower ties, but he never felt the need to enforce a dress code. That's not to say it doesn't matter what teachers wear, he adds.

"I couldn't believe it when I saw female teachers wearing jeans," Mr Haigh says. But if you expect teachers to be suited and booted, who should foot the bill? Mr Haigh's daughter, who works in a hotel, receives a £50 clothing allowance. His other daughter, a primary school teacher, does not.

Mike Welsh, headteacher of Goddard Park Primary School in Swindon and vice-president of the National Association of Head Teachers, takes a more relaxed approach to what his staff wear. Beyond a "no jeans" policy, which resulted from a discussion with staff and parents, he treats teachers as professionals who can decide for themselves what they wear.

"You don't have to be dogmatic about how staff dress," he says. "I wear a suit and tie but I don't expect my staff to do the same unless they want to."

In his 23 years as a headteacher, he has only had to talk to a couple of members of staff about what they are wearing, plus a few supply teachers. He explains the no jeans rule at interview stage, and rarely has to refer to it again.

A handful of surveys of private sector workers show that dressing smartly helps create a good impression at interview and even improves promotion prospects, but there is little or no conclusive research in education to suggest that smart teachers fare better.

Rosie Cairns, a teacher at Ridgeway School in Wroughton, near Swindon, was so convinced that what teachers wore mattered that she conducted her own small study at school. She asked certain male and female teachers to smarten up their wardrobe, hair and (for the women) their make-up.

"My research aimed to gauge just how important our appearance in the classroom might be," she says. "I wanted to establish if it has an impact on teaching and learning."

The newly made-up volunteers had an air of self-assurance, she says, and the pupils said they liked the new look and thought it commanded more respect. "Wearing clothes that the pupils themselves might wear, or wearing scruffy or old fashioned garments were clearly a no-no according to pupils," adds Ms Cairns.

Non-verbal communication can determine how receptive pupils are to teachers, Ms Cairns says. Before teachers even open their mouths, judgements will have been made. "Like it or not, people are judged by the way they dress. I believe that dressing professionally sets the tone and can give staff confidence."

Mr Varney of the UCU is critical of this kind of approach. To him, asking staff to dress smartly is to misunderstand the relationship between the teacher and the learner. "Education is not the same as a business, with customers and retailers," he says. "You don't want to look as if you are flogging a second hand car. I'm extremely doubtful that looking the part, which doesn't necessarily mean acting the part, will raise standards."

It is also a question of what is practical. A tie may look good, but not if it ends up in a pot of glue. One headteacher realised this to his peril when a Year 6 pupil grabbed his tie and wouldn't let go. It took two other teachers to finally get the boy to loosen his grip. From then on, ties were banned.

But Ms Smith remains adamant: "How you dress at work is not about comfort, it's about looking smart. We want to raise the aspirations of our pupils, and being well turned out is part of that."

So next time you are told you dress like a teacher, take pride — it may be a compliment.

Passage 2

Before the mid 1860's, the impact of the railroads in the United States was limited, in the sense that the tracks ended at this Missouri River, approximately the center of the country. At the point the trains turned their freight, mail, and passengers over to steamboats, wagons, and stagecoaches. This meant that wagon freighting, stagecoaching, and steamboating did not come to an end when the first train appeared; rather they became supplements or feeders. Each new "end of track" became a center for animal drawn or waterborne transportation. The major effect of the railroad was to shorten the distance that had to be covered by the older, slower, and more costly means. Wagon freighters continued operating throughout the 1870's and 1880's and into the 1890's. Although over constantly shrinking routes, and coaches and wagons continued to crisscross the West wherever the rails had not yet been laid. The beginning of a major change was foreshadowed in the later 1860's, when the Union Pacific Railroad at last began to build westward from the Central Plains city of Omaha to meet the Central Pacific Railroad advancing eastward from California through the formidable barrier of the Sierra Nevada. Although President Abraham Lincoln signed the original Pacific Railroad bill in 1862 and a revised, financially much more generous version in 1864, little construction was completed until 1865 on the Central Pacific and 1866 on the Union Pacific. The primary reason was skepticism that a Railroad built through so challenging and thinly settled a stretch of desert, mountain, and semiarid plain could pay a profit.

Read the passage above and answer the following questions.
11. The major effect of the railroad was _____.
12. The Pacific Railroad bill was completed in 1865. _____ (Y/N/NG)
13. The main reason for the incompletion of the second version of the bill is _____.

Passage 3

There is strong experimental evidence for age discrimination in hiring, at least for entry-level jobs. Recently, I performed a labor market experiment in Boston in which I sent out thousands of resumes for fictitious entry-level female candidates and measured response rate based on date of high school graduation. Among this group, younger applicants, whose date of high school graduation indicated that they were less than 50 years old, were 40 percent more likely to be called back for an interview than were older applicants.

It is difficult to tell whether employment problems are worse for older workers than for other workers when times are bad. The number of discrimination lawsuits increases during times of high unemployment, but this finding by itself does not indicate an increased level of age discrimination. In times of higher unemployment, the opportunity cost to a lawsuit is lower than it is when times are good.

From the employer's perspective, mass layoffs may seem like a good chance to remove a higher proportion of generally more expensive older workers without the worry of being sued. On the other hand, employers may be less likely to remove protected older workers because they still fear lawsuits. One thing we do know is that once an older worker loses a job, he or she is much less likely to find a new job than a younger worker is.

Choose the best answer according to the passage.

14. The labor market experiment in Boston shows that _____
    A. younger male applicants are more likely to be hired than their female counterparts.
    B. age discrimination is quite common in hiring process.
    C. the author collected information by interviewing female applicants.
    D. female applicants who are 50 years old will never have a chance to get a job.
15. What may lead to the increase of discrimination lawsuits during times of high unemployment?
    A. The increase of age discrimination
    B. The decrease of age discrimination
    C. The decrease of opportunity cost to lawsuits
    D. The increase of opportunity cost to lawsuits

Further Reading

Yearning for That Piece of Green Meadow

It was a February day in early spring that I got to know that green meadow.

Everything around the green meadow was tranquil when it discreetly, with youthful vigor, slowly and quietly displayed the color of life, light yellow and soft green, the characteristics of the beginning of this season.

Spring had just renewed; the green meadow, like a long separated friend from a vast sea of faces or a breath of warmth during the freezing days of winter, gave a new life, and the life-loving strength, and courage to a solitary traveler just coming from the severe cold.

The grass seemed to have just been bathed; one or two dewdrops under the spring sun were rolling on the fresh leaves and showed a refraction of crystal-clear brilliance, like glistening pearls. Dewdrops trembled down off the tips of leaves when a breeze brushed over the lakeside. This reminded me of glittering raindrops falling from eaves in the spring rain, with the apricot blossoming and the growing course of life...

I stood for a long time by the shore of the lake, listening to the sound of life, with warm currents filling my heart. Suddenly spring inside me blossomed into luxuriance. I strongly felt that life was waking after being confined for the whole winter, and my heart was penetrated with a brand-new feeling. The persevering inflexibility of that, weak, yet indomitable grass, showed a primitive magnificence and beauty which helped me vividly realize the real essence and true meaning of life.

Afterwards, the thousands of silent and quiet lives began to bustle. And the grass, lifting up their banner of youth, and bathed in the spring breeze, danced cheerfully and sang to their heart's content. My heart, which had dried up for so long, was filled with vitality from the green meadow.

Then, for the whole spring, the green meadow turned to the oasis where I set my heart out for pasture and it brought me the comfort, which diverted me from the vexations of the world. Watching the grass grow stronger and prettier day by day, I recalled a line from Tagore's poems: "Grass, small as thy pace is, thou hath thy own land under thy feet." And I felt I had my feet planted on the solid ground and, like the little grass, owned the earth beneath my feet.

During the snowing days, standing alone by the window, I recited silently Shelley's famous lines that "If winter comes, can spring be far behind?" Watching the pure-white, graceful snowflakes falling in silence from the lead-gray sky, covering gently the withered meadow, I thought that in the coming year, the grass would flourish.

Yet, the meadow that had given me so much comfort has forever disappeared from my life. It disappeared when a path was constructed to the middle of the lake — a process of creating another form of beauty. Before the extermination however, the grass must have struggled for the right to live on! Just like the grass in Chekov's "Prairie": "She said she earnestly wanted to live on, she was still young. She would be more beautiful..."

But in the struggle of great disparity in strength, it was as easy as turning one's hand over to strangle a life. Closing my eyes, I could see those half-dead, withering grass complaining with grief... that they'd never done anything wrong, yet they would be destroyed by man innocently...

I don't know whether those kind road-builders had ever heard the sad complaint of the grass. But I believe that the silent grievance must have been a kind of swan song of life!

Now, the path winds its way to the middle of the lake — leading into the privacy and seclusion. On moonlit nights, the shadows of trees dance in the breeze. When I walk on the path occasionally, thinking of that green meadow and of the grass, where I placed my feelings and I was comforted, I would feel something moving and tragic filling up my heart, as if I were treading on the remains of the grass and hearing the painful groan and sigh of its soul under my feet!

If a soul does exist when a life comes to an end, then, could the soul of the grass be the only one that groans and moans on the earth?

Now, early spring has appeared once more, with flecks of light yellow and soft green silently breeding. After experiencing the double devastation of nature and man, thousands upon thousands of lives will start a new samsara. Although the deceased is out of existence, the living still has to continue struggling for life!

In fact, in final analysis, life, being dynamic or unknown, is nothing but a solemn and stirring process. Yet just because of this solemn and stirring process, "the sun is new everyday!"

Therefore, I often think of the green meadow.

I. Read the passage above and decide whether the statement is true (T) or false (F).

_____ 1. In the fourth paragraph, dewdrops are metaphoric as glistening pearls.

_____ 2. The author realized the real essence and true meaning of life after he saw

          the indomitable grass.
_____ 3. The green meadow was at last destroyed for constructing a railroad.
_____ 4. According to the author, the road constructed on the green meadow is very beautiful nowadays.
_____ 5. When the grass begins to sprout, the color is green.
_____ 6. Dewdrops remind the author of the growing life.
_____ 7. The grass can dance cheerfully and sing freely in the eyes of the author.
_____ 8. The green meadow is a breath of warmth during the freezing days of winter.

II. Group discussion.
1. Why did the author say that life is nothing but a solemn and stirring process? Did you ever have this kind of feeling? Discuss it with your partner.

   _____
   _____

2. Many figures of speech are used in this passage. Can you find out a few and tell what functions they perform?

   _____
   _____
   _____

Unit 3

Expecting Beauty

I climbed the heights above Yosemite Valley, California, in order to see the splendid granite mountain, Half Dome, in its fullest view. Approaching the edge through the woods I was filled with heightened expectation. I saw the ruin of a cabin and my approach caused the alignment of the chimney on this side of the valley with the shorn mountain across the valley. I stopped. Something happened. The stone verticals corresponded, one human-shaped, the other natural. The human site was still engaged in sightseeing. I was on its side. I saw the famous sight through the eyes of the ruin. I had come expecting beauty; I discovered an unexpected dimension to the beauty of the scene.

In this experience I had been seeking the aesthetic. I knew I would find it, for I had seen post cards in advance and was following the trail map. The seeking took considerable effort and time. It was a heavy investment. I was not going for the scientific purpose of studying rock formation, nor was it for the recreational purpose of exercising my limbs in the fresh air, though that exertion added intensity to the experience and was its context. Primarily, I was going for the scenic wonders. No wonder that I would take delight in seeing Half Dome. The expectation elicited the outcome. I was suitably prepared. No distractions of practical consideration — or theoretic — detracted from my concentrated expectancy. Indeed, the world all around me on the climb contributed to the context for my goal. I was on the terrain of Nature in a national park, following the trail to a viewpoint upon a celebrated natural formation. Each step in the climb not only brought me closer but obliged me to sense the altitude. Moving through the thick woods was in anticipatory contrast to the great gap of the valley and the starkness of the treeless granite boulder.

My spirit and my senses were heightened. I was keenly aware of the world, eager to experience it. My senses were willing to be gratified by their fullest exercise. Hence my eye was sharp, but so was my ear and my nose, I was open to experiencing aesthetically. And on the way I did take minor pleasure in a bird's song, a tree's sway, and a cloud's contortion. I was in the world considered as potential aesthetic realm. Any pleasing feature that appeared would be welcomed. And that welcoming mode drew forth pleasing features. A tonic subjective at-homeness with the world pervaded my feelings. I was in the right mood to enjoy Nature.

Then the unexpected happened. I had no thought in reaching the natural heights that a human structure would be present. Normally, I would have avoided any such structure as I directed my steps toward the natural view. In retrospect it makes sense that a service building be present at the trail end. It may have had facilities for visitors and played an interpretive role. But the building was not present when I arrived. It was absent though its ruin was present. And that ruin spoke to my experience as related to what I had come to see. If I had been trudging on in a dulled state, passing the time in surroundings — like those of the railway station — that did not draw interest, I might well have missed the chimney, walked past it as if it were another tree on the way to the goal. The heightened intensity of my sensibility allowed the chimney to be integrated into the experiencing aesthetically. Readiness was all. The extraterrestrial aesthetician would explain that the creature it was observing on the trail was a specimen of an aesthetic being whose experiencing apparatus for the aesthetic was on full alert. The individual was completely given over to the enjoyment of its experience. And while headed in the direction of an anticipated goal it was nonetheless open to enjoying anything that came its way. Something quite unexpected came its way, and it was ready to attend to it, getting the maximum aesthetic value out of the encounter. The creature was embarked on an adventure in experience. Given the wide range of accessible natural wonders in the national park, the individual in the right mood was bound to make gratifying discoveries.

What are the contents of the aesthetic discovery? Formal properties of beauty may be pointed to in what I saw: the verticals as distinctively shaped and gathering space about them, and the interplay between the two kinds of vertical shapes over the enormous intervening space. The pleasure of perspective entered, for though the chimney is miniscule compared to Half Dome, my approaching it from the trail made it assume visual and spatial dignity equal to the mountain. Complexity of human meaning is encountered with poignant irony. The chimney is an enduring marker of the human value placed on the mountain visible from this point. Here human hands raised stones to shelter an experience of pure stone. So I have come to the right place; I am at home. But the human occupation has been lifted; our presence has turned to stone. Nature has reclaimed its elements. Half Dome presides over the petrifaction of the world. Chimney and mountain are in dialogue as I sense the switching between their perspectives. I am present in ruin and in unity.

(Text source: *The Philosophy of Art*, by Robert Ginsberg, 1992.)

Section A: Text-based Reading Comprehension

I. Choose the best answer according to the passage.

1. The author saw all the following things in climbing Half Dome except _____.
   A. the ruin of a cabin
   B. the human-shaped stone
   C. facilities in a service building for visitors
   D. the chimney
2. Which of the following was expected by the author?
   A. The beauty of the mountain Half Dome
   B. A new dimension to the beauty of Half Dome
   C. The ruin on the extreme height of the mountain
   D. The absence of a service building for visitors
3. Why did the author climb the mountain Half Dome?
   A. For scientific study of the rock formation
   B. For recreational purpose in the fresh air
   C. For appreciating scenic wonders
   D. None of the above
4. What's the author's attitude toward the chimney on the mountain?
   A. Favorable   B. Apathetic   C. Antagonistic   D. Uncomfortable
5. All the following words below can describe the author's feelings when he faced the beautiful scenery except _____.
   A. enlightened   B. unexpected   C. joyful   D. curious

II. Answer the following questions.

1. What did the author find during the process of climbing Half Dome?

2. What are the things that the author did not expect to see?

III. Further discussion.

1. If you are going to have a journey, which one would you prefer, natural landscape or historic and cultural heritage?

Unit 3 Expecting Beauty   35

2. Discuss with your team members the benefits and significance of traveling for college students and then present your team's idea to the class with supportive arguments.

_____

_____

Section B: Vocabulary

I. Fill in the blanks with the proper forms of the words given below.

exertion	intensity	elicit	detract	gratify
pervade	retrospect	trudge	integrate	embark
preside	contortion	poignant	approach	endure

1. This unpleasant incident _____ from our enjoyment of the evening.
2. A customs union would _____ the economies of these countries.
3. The minister was asked to _____ at the independence ceremonies of the small island state.
4. We were sweating profusely from the _____ of moving the furniture.
5. In _____, I wish that I had thought about alternative courses of action.
6. It is especially _____ that he died on the day before his wedding.
7. Her praise will _____ all who worked so hard to earn it.
8. He apparently believes his own _____ of the truth.
9. When her knock _____ no response, she opened the door and peeped in.
10. Some forethought and preparation is necessary before you _____ on the project.
11. A very real sense of peace seemed to _____ my whole being.
12. A warmer ocean will change the distribution, frequency, and _____ of hurricanes.
13. Progress was slow as they had to _____ through deep mud.
14. The political system established in 1400 _____ until about 1650.
15. The site is _____ only by sea.

II. Root and word formation.
A. Study the following roots and list more examples in the space provided.

Root	Meaning	Examples	More examples
-tail	to cut	entail, detail	
-tain	to hold	abstain, pertain, sustain	
-teg (tect)	to hide, to cover	detect, protege	
-tend	to stretch	contend, attend, distend	

B. Fill in the blanks with the proper forms of the words given below.

| protect | entail | contain | tend |
| attend | curtail | sustain | detect |

1. Small quantities of poison were _____ in the dead man's stomach.
2. This bottle _____ two glasses of beer.
3. She's always had a _____ to be thin.
4. He raised his arm to _____ his face from the blow.
5. Writing a history book _____ a lot of work.
6. _____ at school is demanded by law.
7. She owes her success to _____ hard work.
8. The government hopes to _____ public spending.

Section C: Cloze

Fill in the blanks with the proper forms of the words given below.

| invariable | besides | confront | acquaint | expect |
| interest | drop | instead | bring | portion |

More months, to the number of twelve, had come and gone, and Mr. Charles Darnay was established in England as a higher teacher of the French language who was conversant with French literature. In this age, he would have been a Professor; in that age, he was a Tutor. He read with young men who could find any leisure and __1__ for the study of a living tongue spoken all over the world, and he cultivated a taste for its stores of knowledge and fancy. He could write of them, __2__, in sound English, and render them into sound English. Such masters were not at that time easily found; Princes that had been, and Kings that were to be, were not yet of the Teacher class and no ruined nobility had __3__ out of Tellson's ledgers, to turn cooks and carpenters. As a tutor, whose attainments made the student's way unusually pleasant and profitable, and as an elegant translator who __4__ something to his work besides mere dictionary knowledge, young Mr. Darnay soon became known and encouraged. He was well __5__, moreover, with the circumstances of his country, and those were of ever-growing interest. So, with great perseverance and untiring industry, he prospered.

In London, he had expected neither to walk on pavements of gold, nor to lie on beds of roses: if he had had any such exalted __6__, he would not have prospered. He had expected labor, and he found it, and did it, and made the best of it. In this, his prosperity consisted.

A certain __7__ of his time was passed at Cambridge, where he read with undergraduates as a sort of tolerated smuggler who drove a contraband trade in European languages, __8__ of conveying Greek and Latin through the Custom-house. The rest of his time he passed in London.

Now, from the days when it was always summer in Eden, to these days when it is mostly winter in fallen latitudes, the world of a man has __9__ gone one way — Charles Darnay's way — the way of the love of a woman.

He had loved Lucie Manette from the hour of his danger. He had never heard a sound so sweet and dear as the sound of her compassionate voice; he had never seen a face so tenderly beautiful, as hers when it was __10__ with his own on the edge of the grave that had been dug for him. But, he had not yet spoken to her on the subject; the assassination at the deserted chateau far away beyond the heaving water and the long, long, dusty roads — the solid stone chateau which had itself become the mere mist of a dream — had been done a year, and he had never yet, by so much as a single spoken word, disclosed to her the state of his heart.

Section D: Reading Skills Training

Directions: The following exercises are meant to improve your fast reading ability. And you are suggested to go over the passages quickly and then answer all the questions within 25 minutes.

Passage 1
For questions 1 – 7, please mark
   Y (for YES) if the statement agrees with the information given in the passage;
   N (for NO) if the statement contradicts the information given in the passage;
   NG (for NOT GIVEN) if the statement is not given in the passage.

For questions 8 – 10, complete the sentences with the information given in the passage.

1. _____ Without her grandmother, Bethany would probably have committed something wrong.
2. _____ According to the national study, grandparents regularly play the role of "parents" in raising the children.
3. _____ According to Ann Buchanan, grandparents should not be deeply involved in their grandchildren's daily care.
4. _____ The main role of grandparents is to take care of their grandchildren's education.
5. _____ According to Jan Furlong's research, a large proportion of grandparents felt isolated from their grandchildren's education.
6. _____ The Buckinghamshire has decided to set up an organization to help grandparents educate their children.
7. _____ Children with the care of their grandparents are likely to suffer less from

adjustment problems.
8. When a family breaks up, grandparents also _____.
9. According to Professor Buchanan, when grandparents play an ever-increasing role, teachers need to recognize the _____ of the wider family in pupils' lives.
10. Bothany used to be in _____ with the police.

Invisible Generation

One in three families depend on grandparents for childcare, especially in times of crisis. But despite their crucial role, few schools cater for the specific needs of these invaluable carers.

If it wasn't for her grandmother, Bethany, 17, would probably be in a young offender's institution by now. She was sleeping rough at 14 after falling out with her parents, and was caught in a cycle of truancy, drinking and fighting. It was her 64-year-old grandmother who took her in, giving her the love and support she needed to get her life back on track.

Without this army of "grand-carers" who step in and fill the parenting gap, especially in times of crisis, schools would have even more disruptive pupils with pastoral problems, a report released this week has found.

Many families would crumble without grandparent involvement, according to a national study commissioned by Grandparents Plus, a charity that champions the role of the UK's 14 million grandparents. In the absence of working or separated parents, they regularly attend school events, provide emotional support, get involved in hobbies or "cheerlead" from the sidelines, it says.

You do not have to look far to see the influence of grandparents at the highest level. Barack Obama may not have become the US President were it not for his grandmother's care and guidance. Madelyn Dunham, who died aged 86 last year, helped to raise Obama. He described her as "the cornerstone of our family" and "the person who encouraged and allowed us to take chances".

Professor Ann Buchanan, the director of the Oxford Centre for Research into Parenting and Children and co-author of the study, is not surprised by the far-reaching influence of grandparents. She had expected those from more disadvantaged families to be more involved, but she found that grandparents from every type of family play an important part in their grandchildren's lives.

"While parents work, grandparents are increasingly filling the parenting role, be it watching plays or sports matches, helping with homework, giving advice or disciplining the children," she says.

One in three families depend on grandparents for childcare, according to figures from the Office for National Statistics in 2007, which Age Concern estimates is worth almost £ 4 billion a year in childcare costs. The support also continues as children get older.

One in every 100 children is living with a grandparent, the Grandparents' Association states, an average of two to four pupils in every primary school. These grand-carers often have to fill several roles in their grandchildren's life, including that of educators. Professor Buchanan's report, My Second Mum and Dad, shows that they are teachers, homework assistants, career advisers and general supporters. About a fifth of the respondents felt that their grandparents played the key role in supporting their schooling.

But despite their crucial involvement, only a minority of schools are actively catering for the specific needs of grand-carers. "Even when they are the key carers, grandparents are still quite an invisible group," says Sam Smethers, chief executive of Grandparents Plus. "Schools aren't always aware of how to help them. If they are to feel comfortable getting involved in their grandchildren's education, they'll need support and advice from the school."

Fulham Cross Girls' School in west London is trying to do more to accommodate its grandparents. It has seen a marked increase in the number of pupils being looked after by their grandparents, especially among its white British pupils. The school has identified this as an area it needs to focus on and develop. A teacher is due to research how the school can better target and support grandparents as part of her masters degree next year.

"The affected children usually have very young parents who can't handle their children, or are divorced or moving overseas," explains Penny Harwood, Fulham Cross's assistant headteacher. "On the whole, we've been really impressed with grandparents' involvement and their level of questioning."

Despite relatively low parental participation at the school, most grand-carers come to parents' evenings and have been on parenting programmes about how better to support their grandchildren at home. They have also attended international evenings as part of the school's language specialism, and have helped with the planning and performance of school plays. "They're good mentors and role models," says Ms Harwood. However, the school decided not to organise "grandparent days" in case they shied away from the attention.

Other schools, such as St Paul's Cathedral School, an independent school in central London, now hold annual grandparents' days in addition to the more traditional parents' day. This year's involved a concert, a tour of the school conducted by pupils, and afternoon tea with some of the teachers.

Measures such as this help grand-carers to feel included, says Professor Buchanan. "A lot of grandparents want to help with homework or guide their grandchild through their options or the exam system, but they don't feel knowledgeable enough to do so," she says. "A little feedback about how they can help make a positive contribution goes a long way."

Yet schools like Fulham Cross and St Paul's are unusual. A large proportion of grandparents feel excluded from their grandchildren's education, according to research conducted by Jan Furlong, a pre-school development worker based in Leeds. Although baby and toddler groups were open to grandparents, some avoided them because they felt too self-conscious about their age.

"Many felt isolated and would appreciate a place they could attend where they could be with other grandparents and talk like grandparents rather than parents," she says. "It also gives them the opportunity to find out about dealing with children's behaviour."

One 67-year-old grandmother from Buckinghamshire says: "I love looking after my daughter's six-year-old and having her after school, but it does get exhausting, I hope my style of care is right, but I'm not sure if it's in keeping with modern ideas about bringing up children, or helping her develop educationally."

Grandparents like this will need extra teacher support if they are to be called upon to provide some, or all, of the caring responsibilities in the future, especially as parents try to make ends meet during tough economic times. For the three months leading up to June 2007, almost 72 per cent of married and cohabiting mothers were in employment, as were 57 per cent of single parents, according to the latest Labour Force Survey.

Some of these working parents will be both time and money-poor, argues Professor Buchanan. Others will be struggling with alcohol or drug dependency, or drifting in and out of crime.

Of the 1,596 young people between 11 and 16 who responded to the Grandparents Plus report, more than three quarters had experienced two or more adversities in the past year, such as a death in the family, mental health problems or parents in prison. Children who are close to their grandparent are less likely to suffer from adjustment problems during these difficult times, it states.

"Grandparents protect children from the problems they face," says Professor Buchanan. "If parents screw up in some way, they'd much rather go to their grandparents than go into foster care."

One anonymous teacher confirms that an increasing number of parents at her inner-city secondary school are ill-equipped to look after their children, let alone support their education.

"Some of the parents are drug addicts and bail out of parenting altogether," she says. "It's often the grandparents who pick up the pieces, but they can have trouble laying down the law.

"They may tell the child what to do, but the child refuses, saying, 'You're not my mum'. They need help with how to handle that."

Grandparents also make a difference when a family splits. "There used to be a cousin or aunt round the corner who could step in, but now there's less family nearby who can be drawn on in a crisis. The ones with a grandparent round the corner are the lucky ones."

As grandparents play an ever-increasing role, teachers need to recognise the growing impact of the wider family in pupils' lives, argues Professor Buchanan. "It would be helpful to see grandparents as a second set of parents as opposed to an inconvenient add-on," she says.

The rewards will be far-reaching. Grandparents who get involved with their grandchildren are more likely to be "pro-social" (sociable), according to the Grandparents Plus report. Those who got "stuck in" with their grandchildren's life and education found they were more considerate and sensitive.

"They are generally nicer kids when their grandparents are involved," says Professor Buchanan. "They are less likely to have antisocial problems or Asbos." Bethany's experience supports this. She used to be in constant trouble with the police. Now she is studying public services at college and hopes to join the Forces once she's finished.

She has received support from many different sources, including her mother, school and the youth offending team. But she is convinced that it was her grandmother's loyalty and devotion that really saw her through.

Passage 2

I have known very few writers, but that I have known, and whom I respected, confess at once that they have little idea where they are going when they first set pen to paper. They have a character, perhaps two; they are in that condition of eager discomfort which passes for inspiration; all admit radical changes of destination once the journey has begun; one, to my certain knowledge, spent nine months on a novel about Kashmir, then reset the whole thing in the Scottish Highlands. I never heard of anyone making a "skeleton", as we were taught at school. In the breaking and remaking, in the timing, interweaving, beginning afresh, the writer comes to discern things in his material which were not consciously in his mind when he began.

This organic process, often leading to moments of extraordinary self-discovery, is of an indescribable fascination. A blurred image appears, he adds a brushstroke and another, and it is gone; but something was there, and he will not rest till he has captured it. Sometimes the yeast within a writer outlives a book he has written. I have heard of writers who read nothing but their own books, like adolescents they stand before the mirror, and still cannot fathom the exact outline of the vision before them. For the same reason, writers talk interminably about their own books, winkling out hidden meanings, superimposing new ones, begging response from those around them.

Read the passage above and answer the following questions.
11. The organic process is to indicate the condition of eager discomfort of writing. _____ _____ (Y/N/NG)
12. It is easy for writers to be familiar with their own works. _____ (Y/N/NG)

Passage 3

Has the quality of our lives at work, at home and in our communities increased in direct proportion to all the new Internet and business-to-business Internet services being introduced into our lives? I have asked this question of hundreds of CEOS and corporate executives in Europe and the United States. Surprisingly, virtually everyone has said, "No, quite contrary." The very people responsible for ushering in what some have called a "technological renaissance" say they are working longer hours, feel more stressed, are more impatient, and are even less civil in their dealings with colleagues and friends — not to mention strangers. And what's more revealing, they place much of the blame on the very same technologies they are so aggressively championing.

The techno gurus promised us that access would make life more convenient and give us more time. Instead, the very technological wonders that were supposed to liberate us have begun to enslave us in a web of connections from which there seems to be no easy escape.

If an earlier generation was preoccupied with the quest to enclose a vast geographic frontier, the .com generation, it seems, is more caught up in the colonization of time. Every spare moment of our time is being filled with some form of commercial connection, making time itself the scarcest of all resources. Our e-mail, voice mail and cell phones, our 24-hour Interact news and entertainment all seize for our attention.

Read the passage above and answer the following questions.
13. People often blame for the same technology for similar reasons. _____ (Y/N/NG)
14. With technological wonders, we have made life much easier and more convenient. _____ (Y/N/NG)
15. The author is negative to the "technological renaissance" and the. com generation. _____ (Y/N/NG)

Further Reading

Oscar Wilde: The Philosophy of Beauty

The greatest claim that Oscar Wilde made for himself was that he was a high priest of aesthetics that he had a new message concerning the relations of beauty and the worship of beauty to life and art, to life and to morals to give to the world. This claim was one in which to the last he pathetically believed. He was absolutely certain in his own mind that this was his vocation. He elaborated a sort of philosophy of beauty which not only pleased and satisfied himself, but found very many adherents, and became the dogma of a school.

Even in this last work, *De Profundis*, ("the depth of misery") written in the middle of his degradation and misery, he still believes that it is by art that he will be able to regenerate his spirit. He said that he would do such work in the future, would build beautiful things out of his sufferings that he might cry in triumph "Yes! This is just where the artistic life leads a man."

We all know where the artistic life did lead Oscar Wilde upon his release from prison. It led him to an obscure quarter of Paris where he dragged out the short remainder of an unhappy life, having written nothing save *The Ballad of Reading Gaol*, and becoming more and more lost to finer aspirations.

Yet, nevertheless, this aesthetic philosophy of Wilde's forms one of the most important parts of his writings, and of his attitude towards life. It must, therefore, be carefully considered in any study of the man and his work.

First of all, let us inquire, what are aesthetics? Do not let anyone who has not given his attention to the subject imagine that the "aestheticism," which became known as the hallmark of a band of people led by Oscar Wilde who committed many whimsical extravagances, and who were caricatured in Mr. Gilbert's "Patience," has any relation whatever to the science of aesthetics. Even to Oscar Wilde, aestheticism, as it has been popularly called, was only the beginning of an aesthetic philosophy which he summed up finally much later in *Intentions*, the *Poems in Prose*, and *The Soul of Man under Socialism*.

By aesthetics is meant a theory of the beautiful as exhibited in works of art. That is to say, aesthetics considered on its objective side has to investigate, first, a function of art in general as expressing the beautiful, and then the nature of the beauty thus expressed.

Secondly, the special functions of the several arts are investigated by aesthetics and the special aspects of the beautiful with which they are severally concerned. It, therefore, follows that aesthetics has to discuss such topics as the relation of art to nature and life, the distinction of art from nature, the relation of natural to artistic beauty, the conditions and nature of beauty in a work of art, and especially the distinction of beauty from truth, from utility, and from moral goodness.

Aesthetics is, therefore, not art criticism. Art criticism deals with this or that particular work or type of art, while the aesthetic theory seeks to formulate the mere abstract and fundamental conceptions, distinctions, and principles which underlie artistic criticism, and alone make it possible. Art criticism is the link between aesthetic science and the ordinary intelligent appreciation of a work of art by an ordinary intelligence. Much more may be said in defining the functions of aesthetics, but this is sufficient before we begin to examine Wilde's own aesthetic theories.

His ideas were promulgated in the three works mentioned above, and also given to the world in lectures which he delivered at various times.

It is true, as Mr. Arthur Symons very clearly pointed out some years ago, that Oscar Wilde wrote much that was true, new, and valuable about art and the artist. But in everything that he wrote he wrote from the outside. He said nothing which had not been said before him, or which was not the mere willful contrary of what had been said before him. Indeed, it is not too much to say that Oscar Wilde never saw the full face of beauty. He saw it always in profile, always in a limited way. The pretence of strict logic in Wilde's writing on "Artistic Philosophy" is only a pretence, and severe and steady thinkers recognize the fallacy.

Let us examine Oscar Wilde's aesthetic teaching.

In one of his lectures given in America he said —

"And now I would point out to you the operation of the artistic spirit in the choice of subject. Like the philosopher of the platonic vision, the poet is the spectator of all time and all existence. For him no form is obsolete, no subject out of date; rather, whatever of life and passion the world has known in the desert of Judea or in Arcadian valley, by the ruins of Troy or Damascus, in the crowded and hideous streets of the modern city, or by the pleasant ways of Camelot, all lies before him like an open scroll, all is still instinct with beautiful life. He will take of it what is salutary for his own spirit, choosing some facts and rejecting others, with the calm artistic control of one who is in possession of the secret of beauty. It is to no avail that the muse of poetry be called even by such a clarion note as Whitman's to migrate from Greece and Ionia and to placard 'removed' and 'to let' on the rocks of the snowy Parnassus. For art, to quote a noble passage of Mr. Swinburne's, is very life itself and knows nothing of death. And so it comes that he who seems to stand most remote from his age is he who mirrors it best, because he has stripped life of that mist of familiarity, which, as Shelley used to say, makes life obscure to us.

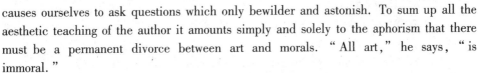

"In the primary aspect a painting has no more spiritual message than an exquisite fragment of Venetian glass. The channels by which all noble and imaginative work in painting should touch the soul are not those of the truths of lives. This should be done by a certain inventive and creative handling entirely independent of anything definitely poetical in the subject, something entirely satisfying in itself, which is, as the Greeks would say, in itself an end. So the joy of poetry comes never from the subject, but from an inventive handling of rhythmical language."

In "Intentions" he enunciated serious problems which seemed constantly to contradict themselves, and he causes ourselves to ask questions which only bewilder and astonish. To sum up all the aesthetic teaching of the author it amounts simply and solely to the aphorism that there must be a permanent divorce between art and morals. "All art," he says, "is immoral."

Some people have taken the view that Oscar Wilde in his philosophy of beauty was never quite sincere. He did not write for philistines with his heart in his mouth, but merely with his tongue in his cheek. I remember Mr. Richard Le Gallienne once said that in "Intentions" Wilde's worship of beauty, which had made a latter-day myth of him before his time, was overlaid by his gift of comic perception, and, rightly viewed, all his flute-tone periods were written in the service of the comic muse. When he was not of malice aforethought humorous in those parts of the work where he seems to be arguing with a serious face enough, it is implied that he did so simply that he might smile behind his mask at the astonishment of a public he had from the first so delighted in shocking that he had a passion for being called "dangerous," just as one type of man likes to be called "fast" and a "rake."

This is, of course, one point of view, but it is not one with which I am in agreement. Wilde laid such enormous stress upon the sensuous side of art, and never realized that this is but an exterior aspect which is impossible and could not exist without a spiritual interior, an informing soul.

With all his brilliancy the author of "Intentions" only saw a mere fragment of his subject. It may be that he willfully shut his eyes to the truth. It is more likely that he was incapable of realizing the truth as a whole, and that what he wrote he wrote with absolute sincerity.

It has been said that the artist sees farther than morality. This is a dangerous doctrine for the artist himself to believe, but it has some truth in it. In Oscar Wilde's case, in pursuing the ideal of beauty he may have seen "farther than morality," but blind of one eye he missed Morality upon the way and did not realize that she was ever there.

I. Read the passage above and decide whether the statement is true (T) or false (F).

_____ 1. Wilde's ideas are embodied mainly in three works: *Intentions*, *Poems in Prose* and *The Soul of Man under Socialism*.

_____ 2. The author thought that Wilde has seen the full face of beauty.

_____ 3. Mr. Swinburne held the opinion that he who seems to stand most remote from his age is he who mirrors it best.

_____ 4. The author disagreed with Wilde's laying too much stress upon the sensuous side of art.

_____ 5. Wilde considered that there must be a permanent divorce between art and morals.

_____ 6. Aestheticism was actually not an aesthetic philosophy at all.

_____ 7. Wilde thought that all things lie before a poet like an open scroll and are important for him to write.

_____ 8. Oscar Wilde's philosophy of beauty was the dogma of a school.

II. Research and Mini-presentation:

Oscar Wilde is known for his involvement in the aesthetic movement based on the principle of *art for art's sake*. So, what did you know about him and his view on art? Do some researches in the library or on the Internet, and present your findings and thoughts to the class.

Topic 2   Religion

Religion is an organized collection of beliefs, cultural systems, and world views that relate humanity to the supernatural, and to spirituality. Many religions have narratives, symbols, and sacred histories that are intended to create meaning to life or traditionally to explain the origin of life or the Universe. From their beliefs about the cosmos and human nature, they tend to derive morality, ethics, religious laws or a preferred life style. According to some estimates, there are roughly 4,200 religions in the world.

Religious activities around the world

Many religions may have organized behaviors, clergy, a definition of what constitutes adherence or membership, holy places, and scriptures. The practice of a religion may also include rituals, sermons, commemoration or veneration of a deity, gods or goddesses, sacrifices, festivals, feasts, trance, initiations, funerary services, matrimonial services, meditation, prayer, music, art, dance, public service or other aspects of human culture. Religions may also contain mythology.

The word religion is sometimes used interchangeably with faith, belief system or sometimes set of duties; however, in the words of émile Durkheim, religion differs from private belief in that it is "something eminently social". A global 2012 poll reports that 59% of the world's population is religious, and 36% are not religious, including 13% who are atheists, with a 9 percent decrease in religious belief from 2005.

Selected words on religion:

Christianity	基督教	Islamism	伊斯兰教
Catholicism	天主教	Buddhism	佛教
Taoism	道教	Judaism	犹太教
atheism	无神论	monotheism	一神论
polytheism	多神论	pantheism	泛神论

Unit 4

Bound to Be Free

At the end of the popular movie *Brave Heart*, just before being beheaded, the Scottish hero William Wallace utters his last word: "Freedom." In light of this cruel ending, many might want to respond with a sigh of relief and a sense of pride: "I'm proud to be an American, where at least I know I'm free" — a statement that can be variously applied to any other modern democracy. In modern democracies we usually need not fear that we might be beheaded when we fight for our own freedom or for that of others. And this surely is one great thing about freedom.

Yet we profoundly deceive ourselves when we stop there in thinking about freedom. Why? Because, strangely enough, there are worse things that can happen to us than being beheaded. We need to ask more rigorously: What is so great about freedom? And we must also ask about the nature of freedom. What do we mean when we talk about freedom? And who has this freedom?

In our day-to-day thinking we tend to confuse three levels of freedom. We tend to think first of political freedom: the freedom of *Brave Heart*, the freedom that was at stake in the American Revolution — that is, Jefferson's, Franklin's and Washington's freedom, and by extension the freedom sought by Rosa Parks and Martin Luther King Jr.

When we reflect a bit longer on the topic, we arrive at a second kind of freedom, the kind that is the presupposition of political freedom: moral freedom. This is the freedom on the grounds of which we are morally responsible. Moreover, according to the principles of Enlightenment political thinking, only truly autonomous — that is to say, free — persons can be entrusted with the complex project of political self-governance.

Modern thinking about freedom stops at the point of autonomy (postmodern thinking despairs long before). Yet in order to grasp what is so great about freedom we have to push beyond Kantian autonomy to a third level, where we find ourselves in the strange but exhilarating company of people like Augustine, Thomas Aquinas and Martin Luther, Jonathan Edwards and Soren Kierkegaard, Karl Barth and Edith Stein, while they all agree that it is this third level of freedom that is most fundamental and decisive: the freedom of living with God.

It is at this level of freedom that all freedom stands or falls. This third, most fundamental level addresses the question, what constitutes the human as human? What makes us who we essentially are?

The epoch of modernity defined itself by rejecting Christianity's answer to the question, what is so great about freedom? Goethe's famous poem *Prometheus* captures the modern answer: what is great about freedom is moral sovereignty and self-sufficiency. By heroically defying the gods, Prometheus claims freedom for himself and the whole human race. Moreover, he shows that freedom makes him Prometheus in the first place: "Here I sit, forming men / In my own image, / A race, that is like me, / Made to suffer, to weep, / To take pleasure and to enjoy itself, / And to pay no attention to your kind, / Like me." I call this perspective, in which the Promethean "I" imagines itself as sovereign, the modern daydream.

Having been foreshadowed in various ways for about 150 years, the modern daydream of the sovereign self came to full bloom at the end of the 18th century. What had happened? A disastrous and deeply pretentious "exchange of attributes" between God and humanity had occurred: freedom for contingency. Humanity had usurped libertas (a Latin word, referring to the ancient Roman personification of liberty) the full and ungrounded freedom of sovereignty. For Luther and previous orthodox Christian theologians, sovereignty had been solely a divine attribute. In the modern period, in exchange for sovereignty, humanity handed over to God contingency, the essential attribute of what it means to be a creature. The world was now thinkable without God. Like Prometheus, humanity was now completely its own sovereign.

It did not take long for the nihilistic implications of this usurpation of divine sovereignty to be felt. God not only became contingent but was even pronounced dead. This move is the presumptuous last consequence of modernity's answer to what is so great about freedom: God is dead and the human is divine.

In humanity's utmost presumption lies the seed of the fall from the modern daydream of freedom into the postmodern nightmare of freedom. It is important to remember that part of the modern daydream was a fundamental exchange of juridical positions between God and humanity, that is, between bench and dock.

During reason's trial of God, the god of the deists died in the dock. And with this god dead, only humankind is left to blame for the miseries that we inflict upon each other. Theodicy turns into anthropodicy. That is, in the face of evil and suffering, it is now humanity, instead of God, that needs to be acquitted. Moreover, the nature of salvation has changed. If we don't save the world, no one else will. Progress has turned from an optimistic possibility into a sheer necessity. If we don't decide and thus choose who we are or what we want to be and do, some other human will. In Jean-Paul Sartre's famous dictum: "We are condemned to be free."

Faced with the infinite responsibility that accompanies the claim of infinite freedom, the Promethean self loses its nerve, capitulates, and flees from the posture of heroic sovereignty into the self-deceptive camouflage of petty license. License promises ultimate relief, because it allows the exhausted and overextended modern self to let its desires rule without accountability. "Freedom" now means living out whatever drives us. Such freedom, however, is eventually exposed as a life that consists in nothing other than the search for the next sensual pleasure.

What does all this mean? Whenever "freedom" becomes simply an issue and a catchword, limited to the political and moral levels, and especially when it is reduced simply to license, we become dangerously oblivious to the fundamental crisis of freedom that threatens humanity. Our concern for political and moral freedom in the face of the real crisis of freedom resembles a homeowner's preoccupation with a fire in the backyard trash can while her house burns down behind her.

In the midst of the presumptuous "public sphere" daydream of cloning humans and tinkering with the human genetic code — not to mention the unchallenged "private sphere" supremacy of license — we may simply lose the ability to ask what is so great about freedom and still expect an answer that truly liberates and transforms our lives.

We should have a serious look again at Aldous Huxley's prophetic novel *Brave New World*. We find there hauntingly displayed how license and genetic programming go together: the late modern subject understands itself to be at once completely "free" and completely "determined." Then we will start to understand that we have come to the brink of denying human freedom and dignity on its most fundamental level, a denial that ultimately encompasses moral and political freedom as well.

How can we open ourselves to a truthful answer to the question about freedom? How can we gain access to an answer that truly liberates and transforms? We must start by allowing ourselves to be awakened from both the daydream and the nightmare. And waking happens first by hearing.

It was common consensus for centuries of Christian thinking that creation's whispering sound has always already been around us and in us, addressing us constantly in the sheer fact of creation. Our being God's creatures, that is, our being constantly dependent on the Creator and called to acknowledge the Creator in gratitude, is thus an evident truth — yet one from which we have fled into daydreams and nightmares. Even though creation ceaselessly addresses us, our dull ears need a stronger signal, God's own waking call, God's own Word become incarnate.

The Christian insight into freedom is that genuine freedom is an original gift of God. Martin Luther expresses this insight in his commentary on Genesis 2, which he sees as a portrayal of the fundamental human predicament. Luther assumes that humanity was originally created for a freedom grounded in an intense and joyful communion with God, a communion that receives its proper creaturely form by following God's commandment. For Adam, says Luther, genuine freedom and God's commandment stand in no contradiction to each other. Rather, God's commandment gives concrete creaturely shape to genuine freedom. In breaking God's original commandment, humanity abandoned the very form of genuine, received freedom and lost the original communion with God. Only then did the commandments turn into the law that both constrains and unmasks the human pretension to self-grounding. Only then did God's law turn into the yoke that only Christ can lift.

In Christ the triune God restores the original communion as a gift received by faith alone through Christ's self-donation on the cross, thereby fulfilling the law in an exemplary way and granting life in God's spirit of love, the law is abrogated through Christ insofar as it constrains, unmasks and convicts the sinner. Since sin, however, is still present in the life of the Christian, the law continues to unmask sin, keeping the believer focused on the need to continuously receive the gift of Christ's self-giving that constitutes genuine freedom. In short, an ongoing struggle continues in every Christian between flesh and Spirit.

Yet this struggle must not be conceived as a static dialectic, an unending back-and-forth between sin and forgiveness, but must be seen as a dynamic — whose subject and agent is Christ through the Spirit — that results in an ongoing growth in faith. It is on this basis that God's commandment, God's law, can become a source of genuine delight — which is the enactment of genuine freedom.

Thus the law's content is restored to its original intent as the genuine expression of God's will: the law of love. It provides the creaturely form of genuine freedom, the freedom of communion with God as received by faith. Now it is God's own law of love received in Christ, a law therefore welcomed with delight: "Whenever there is this delight, it does what God commands. Then the law does not cause a guilty conscience, but causes joy, because one has become another person already" (Luther).

Genuine freedom comes only when it is received by faith. There is no other source. Genuine freedom grows out of the restored and redeemed relationship with the One who, as Luther put it so memorably in his Small Catechism, "has created me together with all that exists." The very heartbeat and life of this relationship and thus of true freedom is love, the caritas created by the Holy Spirit in the human heart.

(Text source: *Bound to Be Free* by Reinhard Hütter, 2004.)

Section A: Text-based Reading Comprehension

I. Choose the best answer according to the passage.
1. At the end of the 18th century, which one of the following statements was not considered to be correct?
    A. The notion of sovereignty became popular.
    B. Humanity had taken the place of absolute sovereignty.
    C. Sovereignty was not merely a divine attribute.
    D. The world was unthinkable without god.
2. Which one of the following is false according to the passage?
    A. Christians are deeply instilled that they are created by God.
    B. For Martin Luther, Christians' genuine freedom accorded with God's commandment.
    C. Human sin and God's law was in a permanent struggle.
    D. For Christians, humanity can be independent of the communion with God.
3. How is genuine freedom accomplished according to the author?
    A. By believing in genuine delight
    B. By loving every people
    C. By faith

D. By self-sufficiency and moral sovereignty
4. Which one is not included in the three levels of freedom according to the author?
   A. The freedom that is at stake in the American Revolution
   B. The freedom on the grounds of which we are morally responsible
   C. The freedom of Prometheus
   D. The freedom of living with God
5. Which one of the following is not a consequence of the trial of God?
   A. The god of deists was dead.
   B. God needs to be acquitted.
   C. Human beings are responsible for their own miseries.
   D. The nature of salvation has changed.

II. Answer the following questions.
1. Why does the author mention Goethe's famous poem *Prometheus* in this passage?

2. What does the author mean by the statement "Theodicy turns into anthropodicy"?

III. Further discussion.
1. What does the author mean by the statement that "Our concern for political and moral freedom in the face of the real crisis of freedom resembles a homeowner's preoccupation with a fire in the backyard trash can while her house burns down behind her"?

2. "Genuine freedom comes only when it is received by faith." To what extent do you agree or disagree with this statement? And why?

Section B: Vocabulary

I. Fill in the blanks with the proper forms of the words given below.

profound	behead	exhilarate	constitute	defy
foreshadow	acquit	capitulate	constrain	eclipse
abrogate	incarnate	dictum	contingency	haunt

1. These acts _____ interference in the internal affairs of other countries.
2. Both governments voted to _____ the treaty.
3. This was the first time that I dared to _____ my mother.
4. The writer's name remained in _____ for many years after his death.
5. The truth of the _____ has been demonstrated in history, both ancient and recent, time and again.
6. The kidnappers had threatened to _____ all four unless their jailed comrades were released.
7. The enemy was warned to _____ or face annihilation.
8. His strong left-wing views make him the devil _____ to more extreme Conservatives.
9. The _____ erudition of the writer came from long years of study.
10. These tastes and incomes _____ how the quantity demand will react to changes in price.
11. The disappointing sales figures _____ more redundancies.
12. Five months ago he was _____ on a shoplifting charge.
13. I need to examine all possible _____.
14. This dangerous task _____ his spirits.
15. This was about 16 years ago, but I still remember its _____ beauty.

II. Root and word formation.
A. Study the following roots and list more examples in the space provided.

Root	Meaning	Examples	More examples
-nomin (nomen)	name	nominal, nominate	
-nov	new	renovate, novel	
-onym (onom)	name, word	anonymous, synonym	
-op (opt)	eye	optional, optic	

B. Fill in the blanks with the proper forms of the words given below.

| nominate | myopic | renovate | innovation |
| anonymous | nominal | optional | novel |

1. The government still has a(n) _____ attitude to spending.
2. The old man is only the _____ head of the business; his daughter makes all the decision.
3. It is unpleasant to receive _____ letters.
4. By this Sunday I will finish _____ an old house.
5. The _____ of air travel during this century has made the world seem smaller.
6. The president _____ me as his representative at the meeting.
7. English is compulsory for all students, but art and music are _____.
8. They mistook _____ for originality, creativity, and competence.

Section C: Cloze

Fill in the blanks with the proper forms of the words given below.

| during | for | until | share | according |
| effect | never | tend | whom | get |

The greatest recent social changes have been in the lives of women. __1__ the twentieth century there has been a remarkable shortening of the time of a woman's life spent in caring __2__ children. A woman marrying at the end of the nineteenth century would probably have been in her middle twenties, and would be likely to have seven or eight children, of __3__ four or five lived till they were five years old. By the time the youngest was fifteen, the mother would have been in her early fifties and would expect to live a further twenty years, during which custom, opportunity and health made it unusual for her to __4__ paid work. Today women marry younger and have fewer children. Usually a woman's youngest child will be fifteen when she is forty-five years and is likely to take paid work __5__ retirement at sixty. Even while she has the care of children, her work is lightened by household appliances and convenience foods.

This important change in women's life-pattern has only recently begun to have its full __6__ on women's economic position. Even a few years ago most girls left school at the first opportunity, and most of them took a full-time job. However, when they married, they usually left work at once and __7__ returned to it. Today the school-leaving age is sixteen, many girls stay at school after that age, and though women __8__ to marry younger, more married women stay at work at least until shortly before their first child is born. Very many more afterwards return to full or part-time work. Such changes have led to a new relationship in marriage, with the husband accepting a greater __9__ of the duties and satisfactions of family life and with both husband and wife sharing more equally in providing the money, and running the home, __10__ to the abilities and interests of each of them.

Section D: Reading Skills Training

Directions: The following exercises are meant to improve your fast reading ability. And you are suggested to go over the passages quickly and then answer all the questions within 25 minutes.

Passage 1
For questions 1 – 7, please mark
  Y (for YES) if the statement agrees with the information given in the passage;
  N (for NO) if the statement contradicts the information given in the passage;
  NG (for NOT GIVEN) if the statement is not given in the passage.

For questions 8 – 10, complete the sentences with the information given in the passage.

1. _____ According to the new research, it is more difficult to lose weight if one goes on diet more frequently.
2. _____ The Framingham Heart Study suggests that people who lost 10 percent of their body weight and then gained 10 percent didn't have the risk of heart disease.
3. _____ Your basal metabolic rate (BMR) will increase during a severe dieting in order to protect your body.
4. _____ Although they keep on their diet along with exercise, most people in our program were likely to "hit a wall".
5. _____ The study of weight changes in rats surprisingly shows that it is more difficult for yo-yo dieters to lose weight and much easier to regain the weight loss.
6. _____ A dieter who gains weight back without exercise may regain less fat and more muscle.
7. _____ The best way to achieve permanent weight loss is to eat low-fat, high-complex-carbohydrate diet and do physical exercise regularly.
8. A dieter in a weight-loss program with exercise is not likely to gain the weight back because exercise can help resist _____ .
9. Due to the potential risks of yo-yo dieting, anyone who diets should be especially careful not to _____ .
10. If you want to avoid failure in the diet, you should pay attention to and make plans for _____ .

Getting Thin-for Good

Just about everyone has been on a diet at one time or another, and millions of us have learned that the weight we lose is all too easily regained. Still few people question the wisdom of dieting. After all, we reason, the worst that can happen is that we'll regain the weight we've lost-then we can simply go on a diet again.

But some new research suggests there is a risk: yo-yo dieting may seriously distort the body's weight-control system. The more diets you go on, the harder it may become to lose weight. Even worse, new evidence indicates that repeated cycles of losing and gaining weight may raise the risk of heart problems.

This last possibility is especially disturbing. As part of a 25 – year study that monitored 1959 men, researchers at the University of Texas School of Public Health in Houston reported in March 1987 that the men showing large up-and-down weight changes had twice the risk of heart disease as those with only small changes in weight. One paper from the Framingham Heart Study, which has monitored more than 5000 people for 40 years, also provides troubling information: people who lost ten percent of their body weight had about 20 percent reduction in risk of heart disease; but people who gained 10 percent raised the risk by 30 percent. These numbers further suggest that going from 150 to 135 pounds, and back to 150 again, could leave you with a higher heart-disease risk than you started with.

When you cut calories and lose weight, your body will protect itself by reducing your basal metabolic rate (BMR). This is the measure of the energy used for routine functions such as breathing and cell repair-roughly 60 to 75 percent of the energy consumed by the body. During severe dieting, your BMR drops within 24 hours and can decline a full 20 percent within two weeks. This metabolic decline is one reason dieters often reach a steady unchanging period, and find that the same caloric intake which melted pounds earlier now produces no weight loss.

The body adapts to dieting in other ways. The enzyme lipoprotein lipase (脂肪酶), a chemical in the body, which controls how much fat is stored in fat cell, may become more active in some overweight people after they have lost weight. That would make the body more efficient at fat storage-exactly what the dieter doesn't want. And this change, like the drop in BMR, may be part of the reason dieters frequently regain their lost weight.

My interest in the yo-yo problem began in 1982, when my colleagues Thomas Wadden and Albert Stunkard and I were experimenting with very-low-calorie diets – 800 calories or fewer per day. We hoped that patients in our clinic could lose large amounts of weight rapidly, then keep the weight loss with a behavior-modification program.

We found, however, that some people lost weight rapidly, some slowly; some lost for a while and then stopped losing. One woman, Marie, began the program at 230 pounds, reduced to 192 pounds, and then " hit a wall", even though she stayed on her diet and walked two miles a day. Marie, like many others in our program, had been a yo-yo dieter, and they tended to have the most difficulty in losing weight.

To see if such dieting could really change the body this way, other researchers and I began to study weight changes in animals. We fed a group of rats a high-fat diet until they became obese. Then we changed their diets repeatedly to make them lose weight, regain, lose again and regain again.

The results were surprising. The first time the rats lost weight, it took 21 days for them to go from obese to normal weight. On their second diet, it took 46 days, even though the rats consumed exactly as many calories.

With each yo-yo, it became easier for the rats to regain. After the first diet, they took 46 days to become obese again; after the second diet, they took only 14 days. In other words on the second yo-yo cycle, it took more than twice as long to lose-weight, and only one-third as long to regain it.

Surprised, our group contacted Harvard surgeon George Blackburn, a pioneer in the use of very-low-calorie diets. Blackburn and his colleagues reviewed the records of 140 dieters who had been through their weight-control clinic, had lost weight and regained it-and had returned for a second try. The records showed the dieters had lost an average of 2.3 pounds a week the first time, but only 1.3 pounds a week the second time.

Four years ago we began the Weight Cycling Project, a major study that includes some of the country's leading obesity researchers. We know that people who lose weight by dieting only and without an exercise program can lose a considerable amount of muscle. But then, if they gain weight back, they may regain less muscle and more fat. While the reason isn't clear, it may be easier for the body to put fat on than to rebuild lost muscle. We're asking if yo-yo dieters may lose fat from one part of the body and regain it elsewhere. For instance, according to our preparatory studies in animals, they could move fat to the abdomen. And research shows that abdominal fat raises the risk of heart disease and diabetes more than fat around the hips and thighs does.

None of this means that dieting is ineffective or foolish. For those who are 20 percent or more overweight, there are good reasons to reduce: successful weight loss can lower blood pressure and cholesterol, help control blood sugar in diabetics and enable people to feel better about themselves. But the new research does suggest that dieting must be taken seriously by people at any weight.

It also means that dieting alone is not the best way to weight control. When a weight-loss program includes exercise, you lose more fat and less muscle, and you're not likely to gain the weight back. That's because exercise may help resist the physiological changes that tend to come from yo-yo dieting.

Given the potential risks of yo-yo dieting, anyone who diets should be especially careful not to gain the weight back. Before you diet, ask yourself how determined you are; then set reasonable goals.

Permanent weight loss should be the main goal, so select a program that will help you change your life-style. Be careful of popular diet programs designed for rapid weight loss and filled with senseless tricks, such as going on and off a diet, eating "magic" foods and so on. A program should focus on sensible changes in nutrition and life-style. The best approach is a low-fat, high-complex-carbohydrate diet and regular physical exercise.

To avoid failing in the diet, recognize and plan for high-risk situations. If you always overeat when you visit your parents, for example, figure out how to get around that before your next visit. Understand that desires-for chocolate, say-are like waves that come up, will quickly subside. When the desire comes, get busy with a simple activity-reading or even brushing your teeth.

Passage 2

Early one morning, more than a hundred years ago, an American inventor called Elias Howe finally fell asleep. He had been working all night on the design of a sewing machine but he had run into a very difficult problem: It seemed impossible to get the thread to run smoothly around the needle.

Though he was tired, Howe slept badly. He turned and turned. Then he had a dream. He dreamt that he had been caught by terrible savages whose king wanted to kill him and eat him unless he could build a perfect sewing machine. When he tried to do so, Howe ran into the same problem as before. The thread kept getting caught around the needle.

The king flew into the cage and ordered his soldiers to kill Howe. They came up towards him with their spears raised. But suddenly the inventor noticed something. There was a hole in the tip of each spear. The inventor awoke from the dream, realizing that he had just found the answer to the problem. Instead of trying to get the thread to run around the needle, he should make it run through a small hole in the center of the needle. This was the simple idea that finally made Howe design and build the first really practised sewing machine.

Elias Howe was not the only one in finding the answer to his problem in this way.

Thomas Edison, the inventor of the electric light, said his best ideas came into him in dreams. So did the great physicist Albert Einstein. Charlotte Bronte also drew in her dreams in writing Jane Eyre.

To know the value of dreams, you have to understand what happens when you are asleep. Even then, a part of your mind is still working. This unconscious (无意识的), but still active part understands your experiences and goes to work on the problems you have had during the day. It stores all sorts of information that you may have forgotten or never have really noticed. It is only when you fall asleep that this part of the brain can send messages to the part you use when you are awake. However, the unconscious part acts in a special way. It uses strange images which the conscious part may not understand at first. This is why dreams are sometimes called "secret messages to ourselves".

11. Elias Howe was the first person who _____.
    A. knew how to solve problems in his dream
    B. was able to design a sewing machine that really worked
    C. was caught by terrible savages
    D. realized the value of dreams
12. Thomas Edison, Albert Einstein and Charlotte Bronte are all mentioned because _____.
    A. they were Howe's best friends
    B. they are all famous inventors
    C. they got some of their ideas in dreams
    D. they all liked dreaming
13. The passage mainly tells us _____.
    A. who designed the sewing machine
    B. how to make a hole in the centre of the needle
    C. how inventions were made
    D. the value of dreams

Passage 3

Reading is the key to school success, and like any skill it takes practice. A child learns to walk by practicing until he no longer has to think about how to put one foot in front of the other. A great athlete practices until he can play quickly, accurately, without thinking. Tennis players call that "being in the zone". Educators call it "automaticity".

A child learns to read by sounding out the letters and decoding (辨识) the words. With practice, he stumbles less and less, reading by the phrase. With automaticity, he doesn't have to think about decoding the words, so he can concentrate on the meaning of the text.

It can begin as early as in the first grade. In a recent study of children in Illinois schools, Alan Rossman of Northwestern University found automatic readers in the first grade who were reading almost three times as fast as the other children and scoring twice as high on comprehension tests. In the fifth grade, the automatic readers were reading twice as far as the others, and still outscoring them on accuracy, comprehension and vocabulary.

"It's not IQ, but the amount of time a child spends reading that is the key to automaticity," according to Rossman. Any child who spends at least 3.5 to 4 hours a week reading books, magazines or newspapers will in all likelihood reach automaticity. At home, where the average child spends 25 hours a week watching television, it can happen by turning off the set just one night favor of reading.

You can test your child by giving him a paragraph or two to read aloud — something unfamiliar but appropriate to his age. If he reads aloud with expression, with a sense of the meaning of the sentence, he probably is an automatic reader. If he reads haltingly, one word at a time, without expression or meaning, he needs more practice.

14. According to the passage, a child with a high IQ doesn't need much practice to be an automatic reader. _____ (Y/N/NG)
15. This passage aims to suggest that automaticity is important for efficient reading. _____ (Y/N/NG)

Further Reading

The Origin of Religion

Where do religions come from?
From the Enlightenment onwards there have been attempts by skeptics to account for religion naturalistically. At first their attention was inevitably focused mainly on Christianity, but later the writings of travelers and anthropologists made it evident that other societies had beliefs and practices that might also be termed religious.

This realization has prompted a lot of speculation about the origins of religion. Why do people in almost all societies seem to believe in the existence of invisible supernatural beings that may influence human life for good or ill and whom it is advisable to pray to or propitiate? And why have almost all societies developed rituals, sometimes very elaborate and demanding in nature, in connection with such beliefs? In spite of much speculation no generally agreed answers to such questions have emerged.

Pascal Boyer's theory
In his recent book *Religion Explained*, the anthropologist Pascal Boyer finds all the hypotheses commonly advanced by rationalists to explain the widespread existence of religion to be superficially plausible but ultimately unsatisfactory. He puts forward instead the theory that religion is the result of psychological mechanisms shared by all normal human minds.

The same systems in the mind that we use to explain everyday occurrences such as a tennis ball breaking a window, he suggests, also generate belief in invisible beings and hidden influences on events. For Boyer there is no real difference between these two sorts of explanatory process. He develops this admittedly counter-intuitive argument at length, with abundant citation of anthropological evidence. An important part of his theory is that the explanatory processes themselves are not accessible to introspection, which is why the beliefs they give rise to are so persuasive. This is an interesting argument though I am not sure that it explains the phenomena fully.

It has often been remarked that there are similarities in the religious ideas of cultures that are widely separated from one another geographically or in time. For Boyer these resemblances are explained by the fact that all human minds and brains function in much the same way. C. G. Jung earlier reached a similar conclusion, though from a different starting point, when he formulated his theory of archetypes. Just as the psychological explanatory mechanisms postulated by Boyer are not accessible to introspection, so with archetypes. We do not have direct access to the archetypes themselves, since they are unconscious, but they may become "constellated" or made manifest at the conscious level in various ways, notably in dreams. (Dreams were considered to be very important in many ancient religious traditions; in the *Bible* Joseph receives Divine guidance in a dream.)

Jung's archetype theory

Some critics have dismissed Jung's archetypes as unscientific and metaphysical, and it is true that there are inconsistencies and obscurities in the way Jung himself described them. However, some modern Jungians, for example Anthony Stevens, have interpreted the idea in a biological sense. Stevens regards the archetypes as inherited patterns of function analogous to instincts in animals. On this view archetypes could be thought of as psychological "instincts" that manifest themselves in behavior and thought patterns.

The widespread devotion to the Virgin Mary in Catholic countries and within Orthodox Christianity can be seen as arising from the archetype of the Anima. Stevens's version of Jung's archetype theory implies that religion is hardwired into the brain. There are (presumably genetic) mechanisms in the brain which tend to give rise to religious experiences and ultimately beliefs.

Richard Dawkins's meme theory

Another idea that has attracted a lot of attention in recent years arises from the concept of memes first introduced by Richard Dawkins almost as an afterthought at the end of his influential popular exposition of modern Darwinism *The Selfish Gene*. Since then, in a kind of recursive illustration of its own hypothesis, meme theory has proliferated enormously so that today we have a "science" of memetics, textbooks on memetics, journals of memetics, websites on memetics, while references to memes constantly appear in books and articles on all kinds of subjects.

Susan Blackmore's view

Dawkins himself has claimed that religions are an example of meme transfer, and the same idea has been developed at some length by Susan Blackmore in her book on memetics. Here she has a whole chapter on the relevance of memes to religion: "Religion as memeplexes".

A memeplex is a group of memes that cooperate to ensure their own survival. So the memes of Catholicism are supposed to include the idea of an omnipotent and omniscient God, the belief that Jesus Christ was the son of God, the Virgin Birth, the infallibility of the Pope, and so on.

Too much emphasis on belief?

This is an attractive idea but I think it attributes too much importance to the role of belief in religion. I want to suggest that the origin of religion is not in belief but in narrative. Religions, I suggest, mostly begin with narrative; belief arises later and is, in a sense, a secondary development.

One can understand why, in a post-Christian context, there should be this emphasis on belief. Belief has always been a central issue in Christianity. Wars have been fought over questions of belief and innumerable heretics have been tortured and burnt for holding what the authorities regarded as incorrect beliefs. Europeans and North Americans therefore tend to assume, as a matter of course, that belief is the fundamental issue in religion. Yet in other religions there has been less emphasis on adherence to particular beliefs. This is certainly true of Hinduism and Buddhism, and even in the other Abrahamic religions, Judaism and Islam, there has been much less persecution of "heretics" than has been the case in Christianity.

Narrative central to religion

Narrative is at the heart of probably every religion we know of. *The Old Testament* is not a philosophical treatise, it is mostly a huge collection of stories and it is on these that its power largely rests. The same is true of the *New Testament*. The narrative of Christ's life, death, and resurrection is intrinsic to Christianity, and Jesus himself used narrative in the form of parables to convey his meaning.

Religion as narrative

One reason why religions have such a strong hold on human societies is that they are based not primarily on intellectual beliefs but on narratives. Story-telling accesses the human psyche not at the intellectual but at the emotional level, where it is more powerful; probably the brain pathways are different for narrative response and belief formation. Human beings are story-telling by nature. Every society seems to have had its story-tellers, its oral epic poets, and the earliest literature that has come down to us (the *Iliad*, the *Odyssey*, the *Gilgamesh* epic) is narrative. Today we still enjoy narratives in the form of plays, films, and novels. (The death of the novel, like the death of religion, is constantly being foretold yet both novels and religions seemingly continue to thrive.)

Intellectual critics today tend to assume that all this narrative material is merely a concession to the limited understanding of the uneducated masses, who are unfitted to understand the sophisticated concepts that are the real substance of religion. I think that this puts things the wrong way round. To understand the appeal of religions we should look first at the narratives in which they are expressed and only subsequently at the doctrinal beliefs that they give rise to.

If this idea is right, it follows that the occurrence of strange beliefs in religion has a ready explanation. Many people find it difficult to distinguish between fact and fiction. Writers of radio or television soap operators often report that people write to the fictional characters in the apparent belief that they are real. This is a trivial illustration of a basic human propensity, which is to project the stories we tell ourselves on the outer world. The human imagination has given rise to religious stories in which all kinds of miraculous and wonderful events occur. These are taken to be real, and give rise to beliefs which are then incorporated into the religions as factual statements.

I. Read the passage above and decide whether the statement is true (T) or false (F).

_____ 1. Boyer thinks that all human minds and brains function in much the same way.
_____ 2. The societies which have beliefs and practices can also be called religious.
_____ 3. Susan Blackmore regards religion as an example of meme transfer.
_____ 4. There have been attempts by critics to describe religion since Renaissance.
_____ 5. Different cultures may have similarities in religious ideas.
_____ 6. We have no access to the archetypes because they are unconscious.
_____ 7. Mimetic derives from a popular exposition of modern Darwinism: *The Selfish Gene*.
_____ 8. According to Boyer, religion is caused by psychological mechanisms which are owned by all normal people.

II. Discussion and mini-presentation.

The author said in the text that human beings are story-telling by nature. Do you agree with it? Discuss with your team members the functions and roles that myth and fairy tales play in our life and then present your team's thoughts to the class.

Unit 5

Is the *Bible* True? (Excerpt)

Whenever there's a really intense fight among American Protestants, sooner or later it seems to turn into an argument over the truth of scripture. At one extreme, some dismiss any appeal to the *Bible* out of hand and consider "authority" a dirty word. Others confidently assert that only their literalistic interpretations really count as believing the *Bible* to be true. Many of us find ourselves wandering around confused in the middle, wanting to believe in the *Bible*, not thinking of ourselves as biblical literalists, but unsure how to characterize our position. Indeed, much of the notorious malaise of mainstream Protestantism derives from a perception that, to the question, "Is the *Bible* true?" The moderate answer is, "Well, sort of . . ." followed by either a lot of confusing talk or an embarrassed silence.

That perception isn't entirely false. Non-fundamentalists' discussions of appeals to the *Bible* have often consisted principally in ridiculing fundamentalism, without defining any clear Christian alternative to fundamentalism. I'm going to try, in limited space, to sketch an alternative way of saying, "Yes, the *Bible* is true."

This claim entails two secondary claims.

First: to say that the *Bible* is true is to say that what it means is true — and what it means is shaped by (among other things) the genres in which the *Bible* is expressed, the attitudes it takes to history, and the ways cultural contexts shaped the meanings of the words that it uses.

Second: to say that this particular book is true is to say that we can trust it, trust it as a guide to faith and life which provides not only specific claims about God's faithfulness and how we ought to live our lives in response to it, but also a way of understanding the whole world and a language in which to speak about that world. These secondary claims may seem a bit complicated, but acknowledging complexity is a way not of hedging commitment to the *Bible*'s truth but of fully attending to the complex ways in which the *Bible* is true.

First, then, let us consider the relation of truth and meaning. It's an obvious point, really — the truth of a statement or a book depends on what it means. Yet the point often gets lost in discussions of biblical truth. Consider the question of genre — the literary term that refers to the kind of work a particular text is. A novel represents a different genre from a work of history, which is different from a lyric poem, and so on. Different genres make different kinds of truth claims.

A work of fiction, for instance, operates differently from a work of history. If David McCullough simply made up some of the episodes recounted in his biography of Harry Truman, then that counts as a fraud — it's not as good a book as we thought was, not to be trusted after all. But if Charles Dickens made up *Oliver Twist*, that doesn't make the novel a lie. Since it belongs to the genre "novel," it isn't supposed to report historical facts accurately.

The distinction between McCullough and Dickens is obvious. To take another example, if we're reading a movie star's autobiography, we assume it will have a more casual relation to the facts than an academic historian's biography of a British prime minister. Different genres have their different rules.

The *Bible* includes a variety of different genres. When we read in Luke's Gospel Jesus' story about the good Samaritan ("A man was going down from Jerusalem to Jericho, and he fell among robbers, who stripped him and beat him, and departed, leaving him half dead") we are not inclined to check the story against the police blotter for the Jerusalem-Jericho highway patrol. We recognize that Jesus is telling a story to illustrate a moral point, and that such stories often don't claim to correspond to actual events.

The opening chapters of Genesis represent a different genre — Karl Barth called it "saga," "an intuitive and poetic picture of a pre-historical reality of history". Events get described which no human being could have witnessed. Animals talk. People live for centuries. We're in a different genre here from that represented by, say, the Gospel narratives of Jesus' last days or the stories of the reign of King David in the Book of *2 Samuel*, which read much more like eyewitness history.

In its intuitive, poetic way, saga communicates truths about the ultimate origins of things, just as the narrative history in the *Bible* presents truth in a different way, stories with a moral lesson like the good Samaritan in another, and the poetry of the Psalms in yet another. "We are," Barth says, "no less truly summoned to listen to what the *Bible* has to say here in the form of saga than to what it has to say in other places in the form of history, and elsewhere in the form of address, doctrine, law, epigram, epic and lyric." But we listen faithfully only when we realize what genre we are encountering.

Texts often provide clues as to their genre. When a story begins, "Once upon a time . . ." we expect a fairy tale. When we flip on the television and see someone saying, "A guy walked up to a man in a bar. . ." we know we're watching a comedy club, not the evening news.

But sometimes, particularly when encountering a text from a different culture, it's hard to recognize the genre. For example, Data, the android on Star Trek, can't recognize jokes. He takes them literally, and often finds himself puzzled.

Another source of confusion in interpreting the *Bible*, or any text that originated in a culture different from our own, lies in the different social conditions of that different time and the ways those conditions give terms different meanings. For instance, slave owners in the American South regularly cited the positive biblical references to slavery to support the ownership of slaves. But slavery in ancient Israel was a very different sort of institution. It was not based on race. Many slaves were supposed to be freed at the end of seven years, and there was a good bit of movement back and forth between slavery and freedom. Israelite slavery may have been a bad institution, but it was a very different institution from that of American slavery. It was more like the hiring of indentured servants, if one wants an American analogy. So one can't simply transfer what the *Bible* says about "slavery" to an American context where the institution and the circumstances are very different and the word therefore has a different meaning.

To understand how the *Bible* is true, therefore, we must understand its genres, recognize its attitudes toward the reporting of historical details, and consider the social context in which it was written. This much could be said about any text of sufficient complexity.

All this makes understanding the *Bible* sound very complicated. It may also seem that the truth of the *Bible* is getting lost in a morass of qualifications. The issues are complicated, but we needn't despair of finding biblical truth because, finally, we can trust the *Bible*. In this respect, Christians read the *Bible* differently from the way they read any other book.

But why should we trust this book in particular? That's a question that admits of no short answer. In part, we trust the *Bible* because we find that it keeps making sense of the world in which we live. Using nearly every genre and every attitude to historical detail imaginable, the *Bible* lays out a richly diverse vision of the world, from beginning to end, and says, in effect, "This isn't some imaginary world, like Tolkien's Middle Earth (the fictional-universe setting of the majority of author J. R. R. Tolkien's fantasy writings). This is the real world, the only one there is. So if you buy into this basic picture of things, then anything real has to fit somewhere into this framework. Your life and the events around you thus will make sense only as they have their place within this grand story."

And Christians find that, if they keep reading this book and live their lives in the context of the community that reads it, that promise keeps getting fulfilled, albeit always tentatively and incompletely. The categories the *Bible* uses, the models it offers for understanding human life and the world around us, and the God about whom it tells can seem at first strange, but we find them ever and again providing clues that put together pieces of our fragmented world in unexpected ways.

Perhaps the most important element in this mix is that we trust the *Bible* because we have come to trust the God about whom it tells us. The process of coming to this kind of trust moves in a kind of circle: we trust in that God in significant part because of what we learn in the *Bible*. It's a mistake to look for a single entry point into this circle. No one doctrine provides the foundation on which we believe all the others. We find ourselves trusting, in the way we sometimes find ourselves in love, without being able to define the steps that led to that state, and the elements that shape our trust are tied together in complicated ways. Even a complete systematic theology will not fully explain such matters, but it follows that we cannot work out even a fairly good doctrine of scripture without, for instance, a doctrine of the Holy Spirit, and then, in turn, a doctrine of the Triune God. If the *Bible* invites us into the world it narrates and describes, it also gives us a language in which to think about the world. The experience of finding yourself thinking in a previously foreign language offers another analogy for what it is like to learn to trust the *Bible*. Moving into a new culture or learning a new skill often involves learning a new language. To understand Japan, I need to learn Japanese. To become a lawyer, I need to learn the vocabulary of the law. When I learn these new languages, I'm not just acquiring a new stock of words; I'm learning to think in a different way.

Christians today often think of their world in the vocabularies of contemporary politics or popular culture. But the *Bible* offers us an alternative. Those poor folk across town are not just "welfare recipients" or even "fellow citizens"; they're "Neighbors". That action wasn't just "inappropriate behavior" or even "crime"; it was "sin." When we use such a vocabulary, we find ourselves thinking about the world in different ways — and sometimes, at least, we may find common ground with other Christians from whom we were divided when our only language was that of contemporary politics.

To trust the *Bible*, to let it define our world and provide a language for thinking about the world, can transform our lives. But it does not make understanding the *Bible* easy. We have to get down to hard work — to reading the *Bible* and immersing ourselves in its world and its language. We need to know the *Bible* well enough so that, as was true for Augustine or Luther or Calvin, one passage reminds us of another that offers a qualification, another that provides support, another that sets out a different frame of reference.

Such immersion in the biblical world and its language leads to much richer interpretation than either quoting proof texts or picking and choosing passages we like. When we really know the *Bible*, we realize its complexities, its diversities, its ambiguities. One of our problems these days, whether we are "liberals" or "fundamentalists," is how few of us can do that. Fundamentalists quote a single proof text to settle the matter, and liberals can't remember any passages at all. If we are to get beyond such a state of affairs, we will have to study the *Bible* much more seriously. But if we believe the *Bible* is true, if we really trust it, we ought to be willing to do the work.

(Text source: *Is the* Bible *True?* by William C. Placher, 1995.)

Section A: Text-based Reading Comprehension

I. Choose the best answer according to the passage.

1. According to the author, which one of the following can't explain the meaning of the claim "Yes, the Bible is true"?
   A. What the *Bible* means is shaped by the genres in which it is expressed.
   B. We can trust the book which was considered as a true one.
   C. We can use it as a way of understanding our world.
   D. We should read it and do as what it asks to do.
2. Which one of the following is not the genre that the *Bible* includes?
   A. Story   B. Saga   C. Song   D. Epic
3. Which one of the following statements is not true?
   A. The *Bible* keeps making sense of the world in which we like and that's why we trust it.
   B. If someone keeps reading the *Bible*, his or her promise may keep getting fulfilled.
   C. The *Bible* not only invites us into the world it narrates and describes, but also influences our way of thinking the world.
   D. The author thinks that the *Bible* is full of complexities, diversities and ambiguities.
4. Which one of the following is not used to show the relationship between genres and truth claims according to the author?
   A. David McCullough's episodes recounted in his biography of *Harry Truman*
   B. Charles Dickens' *Oliver Twist*
   C. The stories of the reign of King David in 2 *Samuel*

D. A movie star's autobiography
5. Which one of the following is not mentioned in terms of how the *Bible* is true?
   A. The genres in which the *Bible* is written
   B. The social context in which the *Bible* is written
   C. The historical background of the roles in the *Bible*
   D. The attitude of the author's reporting historical details

II. Answer the following questions.
1. What does the saying "Yes, the *Bible* is true." entail in the text?
   _____
   _____

2. According to author, what are the main sources of confusion in interpreting the *Bible*?
   _____
   _____
   _____

III. Further discussion.
1. The author claims in the text that "To trust the *Bible*, to let it define our world and provide a language for thinking about the world, can transform our lives." To what extent do you agree or disagree?
   _____
   _____

2. Have you ever read some parts of the *Bible* or stories about the *Bible*? Share your stories with your classmates you have learned from or about the *Bible*.
   _____
   _____

Section B: Vocabulary

I. Fill in the blanks with the proper forms of the words given below.

dismiss	wander	notorious	strip	morass
flip	indenture	albeit	fragment	immerse
ambiguity	tentative	hedge	depart	ridicule

1. It was so hot that we _____ off our shirts.
2. No mathematician is infallible; he may make mistakes, but he must not _____.

Unit 5 Is the *Bible* True? (Excerpt)   73

3. I lost my place in my book when the pages _____ over in the wind.
4. He tried, _____ without success.
5. At first she threatened to _____ me, but later she relented.
6. She was quick to notice the _____ in the article.
7. Do not let the discussion _____ into a desultory conversation with no clear direction.
8. She told us the story of one of Britain's most _____ country house murders.
9. We've made a _____ plan for the vacation but haven't really decided yet.
10. The _____ of rules and regulations is delaying the start of the project.
11. I can see that they are not ready to _____ from traditional practice.
12. The dogs have greater freedom too, for they are allowed to _____ outside their enclosure.
13. The simplest procedure is to _____ the stopper bottle to the required depth.
14. She had to sign a(n) _____ to sell herself, because she owed money to the landlord.
15. She rarely spoke her mind out of fear of being _____.

II. Root and word formation.

A. Study the following roots and list more examples in the space provided.

Root	Meaning	Examples	More examples
-patr (pater)	father, country	paternal, patriarch	
-par (pair)	to arrange	apparel, imperious	
	to appear	apparition, transparent	
	equal	disparity, impair	
-pel (puls)	to drive	dispel, compel, pulse	
-pend	to hang	append, depend	
-portion	share	apportion, portion	

B. Fill in the blanks with the proper forms of the words given below.

patronize	impair	suspense	compel
transparent	dispel	paternal	append

1. Grow the bulbs in a(n) _____ plastic box, so the children can see the roots growing.
2. Her intelligence and skill _____ our admiration.
3. We have been kept in _____ waiting for the examination results.
4. He has a _____ concern for your welfare.
5. It was a relief that his real name hadn't been _____ to the manuscript.
6. Today's attack has seriously _____ attempts to achieve peace in the area.

7. His calm words _____ our fears.
8. The restaurant is _____ by politicians and journalists.

Section C: Cloze

Fill in the blanks with the proper forms of the words given below.

with	while	turn	after	far
amuse	on	by	bestow	into

It was a pretty sight to see the one earnest, sweet-faced girl among the flock of tall lads, trying to understand, to help and please them __1__ a patient affection that worked many a small miracle unperceived. Slang, rough manners, and careless habits were banished or bettered __2__ the presence of a little gentlewoman; and all the manly virtues cropping up were encouraged by the hearty admiration __3__ upon them by one whose good opinion all valued more than they confessed; __4__ Rose tried to imitate the good qualities she praised in them, to put away her girlish vanities and fears, to be strong and just, and frank and brave, as well as modest, kind, and beautiful.

This trial worked so well that when the month was over, Mac and Steve demanded a visit in their __5__, and Rose went, feeling that she would like to hear grim Aunt Jane say, as Aunt Clara did at parting, "I wish I could keep you all my life, dear."

__6__ Mac and Steve had had their turn, Archie and Company bore her away for some weeks; and with them she was so happy, she felt as if she would like to stay forever, if she could have Uncle Alec also.

Of course, Aunt Myra could not be neglected, and, with secret despair, Rose went to the "Mausoleum," as the boys called her gloomy abode. Fortunately, she was very near home, and Dr. Alec dropped in so often that her visit was __7__ less dismal than she expected. Between them, they actually made Aunt Myra laugh heartily more than once; and Rose did her so much good by letting in the sunshine, singing about the silent house, cooking wholesome messes, and __8__ the old lady with funny little lectures __9__ physiology, that she forgot to take her pills and gave up "Mum's Elixir," because she slept so well, after the long walks and drives she was beguiled __10__ taking, that she needed no narcotic.

Section D: Reading Skills Training

Directions: The following exercises are meant to improve your fast reading ability. And you are suggested to go over the passages quickly and then answer all the questions within 25 minutes.

Unit 5 Is the *Bible* True? (Excerpt)   75

Passage 1
For questions 1 –7, please mark
   Y (for YES) if the statement agrees with the information given in the passage;
   N (for NO) if the statement contradicts the information given in the passage;
   NG (for NOT GIVEN) if the statement is not given in the passage.

For questions 8 –10, complete the sentences with the information given in the passage.

1. _____ According to Postel, only one third of the 2.5 percent freshwater on Earth is part of the water cycle.
2. _____ People living in rich countries like the United States couldn't suffer from serious water shortages.
3. _____ The main reasons for current water shortage are population growth and water pollution.
4. _____ A "ghost ship" sinking into the sand, left to rot on dry land by a receding sea is merely a scene from a movie about the end of the world.
5. _____ Scientists studying water in the San Francisco Bay reported in 1996 that 70 percent of the pollutants could be traced to manufacturers.
6. _____ Farmers are also criticized for overusing herbicides and pesticides, chemicals that kill weeds and insects but that pollute water as well.
7. _____ Large-scale efforts to build massive dams and irrigation systems can fix more problems than the problems they result in.
8. In developing countries, the source of pollution mainly comes from _____ people dump into the streams and rivers.
9. Peter H. Gleick worries that as many as one third of the world's people will suffer from _____ by 2025.
10. Water expert Gleick advocates that _____ should make common effort to solve water-related problems.

Will We Run Out of Water?

Picture a "ghost ship" sinking into the sand, left to rot on dry land by a receding sea. Then imagine dust storms sweeping up toxic pesticides and chemical fertilizers from the dry seabed and spewing them across towns and villages.

Seem like a scene from a movie about the end of the world? For people living near the Aral Sea in Central Asia, it's all too real. Thirty years ago, government planners diverted (使转向) the rivers that flow into the sea in order to irrigate (provide water for) farmland. As a result, the sea has shrunk to half its original size, stranding ships on dry land. The seawater has tripled in salt content and become polluted, killing all 24 native species of fish.

Similar large-scale efforts to redirect water in other parts of the world have also ended in ecological crisis, according to numerous environmental groups. But many countries continue to build massive dams and irrigation systems, even though such projects can create more problems than they fix. Why? People in many parts of the world are desperate for water, and more people will need more water in the next century.

"Growing populations will worsen problems with water," says Peter H. Gleick, an environmental scientist at the Pacific Institute for studies in Development, Environment, and Security, a research organization in California. He fears that by the year 2025, as many as one-third of the world's projected 8.3 billion people will suffer from water shortages.

Where Water Goes

Only 2.5 percent of all water on Earth is freshwater, water suitable for drinking and growing food, says Sandra Postel, director of the Global Water Policy Project in Amherst, Mass. Two thirds of this freshwater is locked in glaciers and ice caps. In fact, only a tiny percentage of freshwater is part of the water cycle, in which water evaporates and rises into the atmosphere, then condenses and falls back to Earth as precipitation (rain or snow).

Some precipitation runs off land to lakes and oceans, and some becomes groundwater, water that seeps into the earth. Much of this renewable freshwater ends up in remote places like the Amazon river basin in Brazil, where few people live. In fact, the world's population has access to only 12,500 cubic kilometers of freshwater—about the amount of water in Lake Superior. And people use half of this amount already. "If water demand continues to climb rapidly," says Postel, "there will be severe shortages and damage to the aquatic environment."

Close to Home

Water woes may seem remote to people living in rich countries like the United States. But Americans could face serious water shortages, too especially in areas that rely on groundwater. Groundwater accumulates in aquifers, layers of sand and gravel that lie between soil and bedrock. (For every liter of surface water, more than 90 liters are hidden underground.) Although the United States has large aquifers, farmers, ranchers, and cities are tapping many of them for water faster than nature can replenish it. In northwest Texas, for example, over pumping has shrunk groundwater supplies by 25 percent, according to Postel.

Americans may face even more urgent problems from pollution. Drinking water in the United States is generally safe and meets high standards. Nevertheless, one in five Americans every day unknowingly drinks tap water contaminated with bacteria and chemical wastes, according to the Environmental Protection Agency. In Milwaukee,

400,000 people fell ill in 1993 after drinking tap water tainted with cryptosporidium, a microbe that causes fever, diarrhea and vomiting.

The Source

Where do contaminants come from? In developing countries, people dump raw sewage into the same streams and rivers from which they draw water for drinking and cooking; about 250 million people a year get sick from water borne diseases.

In developed countries, manufacturers use 100,000 chemical compounds to make a wide range of products. Toxic chemicals pollute water when released untreated into rivers and lakes. (Certain compounds, such as polychlorinated biphenyls, or PCBs, have been banned in the United States.)

But almost everyone contributes to water pollution. People often pour household cleaners, car antifreeze, and paint thinners down the drain; all of these contain hazardous chemicals. Scientists studying water in the San Francisco Bay reported in 1996 that 70 percent of the pollutants could be traced to household waste.

Farmers have been criticized for overusing herbicides and pesticides, chemicals that kill weeds and insects but that pollute water as well. Farmers also use nitrates, nitrogen, rich fertilizer that help plants grow but that can wreak havoc on the environment. Nitrates are swept away by surface runoff to lakes and seas. Too many nitrates "over enrich" these bodies of water, encouraging the buildup of algae (海藻), or microscopic plants that live on the surface of the water. Algae deprive the water of oxygen that fish need to survive, at times choking off life in an entire body of water.

What's the Solution?

Water expert Gleick advocates conservation and local solutions to water-related problems; governments, for instance, would be better off building small-scale dams rather than huge and disruptive projects like the one that ruined the Aral Sea.

"More than 1 billion people worldwide don't have access to basic clean drinking water," says Gleick. "There has to be a strong push on the part of everyone— governments and ordinary people—to make sure we have a resource so fundamental to life."

Passage 2

When the German cruise ship Wilhelm Gustloff was hit by torpedoes fired from a Russian submarine in the final winter of World War II, more than 10,000 people — mostly women, children and old people fleeing the final Red Army push into Nazi Germany — were packed aboard. An ice storm had turned the decks into frozen sheets that sent hundreds of families sliding into the sea as the ship tilted and began to go down. Others desperately tried to put lifeboats down. Some who succeeded fought off those in the water who had the strength to try to claw their way aboard. Most people froze immediately. I'll never forget the screams," says Christa Ntitzmann, 87, one of the 1,200 survivors. She recalls watching the ship, brightly lit, slipping into its dark grave — and into seeming nothingness, rarely mentioned for more than half a century.

Now Germanys Nobel Prize-winning author Gtinter Grass has revived the memory of the 9,000 dead, including more than 4,000 children — with his latest novel *Crab Walk*, published last month. The book, which will be out in English next year, doesn't dwell on the sinking; its heroine is a pregnant young woman who survives the catastrophe only to say later: " Nobody wanted to hear about it, not here in the West (of Germany) and not at all in the East. " The reason was obvious. As what Grass put in a recent interview with the weekly Die Woche: " Because the crimes we Germans are responsible for were and are so dominant, we didn't have the energy left to tell of our own sufferings. "

Read the passage above and answer the following questions.
11. The heroine of the novel is given to a pregnant woman because _____.
12. _____ people including _____ children died in this catastrophe.

Passage 3

Petroleum products, such as gasoline, kerosene, home heating oil, residual fuel oil, and lubricating oils, come from one source — crude oil found below the earth's surface, as well as under large bodies of water, from a few hundred feet below the surface to as deep as 25,000 feet into the earth's interior. Sometimes crude oil is secured by drilling a hole through the earth, but more dry holes are drilled than those producing oil. Pressure at the source or pumping forces crude oil to the surface. Crude oil wells flow at varying rates, from ten to thousands of barrels per hour. Petroleum products are always measured in 42 - gallon barrels.

Petroleum products vary greatly in physical appearance: thin, thick, transparent or opaque, but regardless, their chemical composition is made up of two elements: carbon and hydrogen, which form compounds called hydrocarbons. Other chemical elements found in union with the hydrocarbons are few and are classified as impurities. Trace elements are also found, but these are of such minute quantities that they are disregarded. The combination of carbon and hydrogen forms many thousands of compounds which are possible because of the carious positions and joining of these two atoms in the hydrocarbon molecule.

Read the passage above and answer the following questions.
13. Crude oil is always found in dry holes. _____ (Y/N/NG)
14. Crude oil comes from _____.
15. What is not a petroleum product?
    A. Plastics   B. Paraffin   C. Shampoo   D. Lubricant

Further Reading

The Da Vinci Code (Excerpt)

Sophie felt a little chill. "Da Vinci is talking about the *Bible*?"

Teabing nodded. "Leonardo's feelings about the *Bible* relate directly to the Holy Grail. In fact, Da Vinci painted the true Grail, which I will show you momentarily, but first we must speak of the *Bible*." Teabing smiled. " And everything you need to know about the *Bible* can be summed up by the great canon doctor Martyn Percy." Teabing cleared his throat and declared, " The *Bible* did not arrive by fax from heaven."

"I beg your pardon?"

"The *Bible* is a product of man, my dear. Not of God. The *Bible* did not fall magically from the clouds. Man created it as a historical record of tumultuous times, and it has evolved through countless translations, additions, and revisions. History has never had a definitive version of the book."

"Okay."

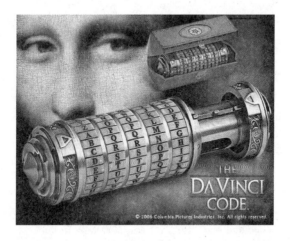

"Jesus Christ was a historical figure of staggering influence, perhaps the most enigmatic and inspirational leader the world has ever seen. As the prophesied Messiah, Jesus toppled kings, inspired millions, and founded new philosophies. As a descendant of the lines of King Solomon and King David, Jesus possessed a rightful claim to the throne of the King of the Jews. Understandably, His life was recorded by thousands of followers across the land. " Teabing paused to sip his tea and then placed the cup back on the mantel." More than eighty gospels were considered for the *New Testament*, and yet only a relative few were chosen for inclusion — Matthew, Mark, Luke, and John among them.

"Who chose which gospels to include?" Sophie asked.

"Aha!" Teabing burst in with enthusiasm. "The fundamental irony of Christianity! The *Bible*, as we know it today, was collated by the pagan Roman emperor Constantine (君士坦丁) the Great."

"I thought Constantine was a Christian," Sophie said.

"Hardly," Teabing scoffed. "He was a lifelong pagan who was baptized on his death bed, too weak to protest. In Constantine's day, Rome's official religion was sun worship — the cult of Sol Invictus (the official sun god of the later Roman Empire and a patron of soldiers), or the Invincible Sun — and Constantine was its head priest. Unfortunately for him, a growing religious turmoil was gripping Rome. Three centuries after the crucifixion of Jesus Christ, Christ's followers had multiplied exponentially. Christians and pagans began warring, and the conflict grew to such proportions that it threatened to rend Rome in two. Constantine decided something had to be done. In 325 A. D. he decided to unify Rome under a single religion. Christianity."

Sophie was surprised. "Why would a pagan emperor choose Christianity as the official religion?"

Teabing chuckled. "Constantine was a very good businessman. He could see that Christianity was on the rise, and he simply backed the winning horse. Historians still marvel at the brilliance with which Constantine converted the sun-worshipping pagans to Christianity. By fusing pagan symbols, dates, and rituals into the growing Christian tradition, he created a kind of hybrid religion that was acceptable to both parties."

"Transmogrification," Langdon said. "The vestiges of pagan religion in Christian symbology are undeniable. Egyptian sun disks became the halos of Catholic saints. Pictograms of Isis (Goddess of health, marriage, and wisdom) nursing her miraculously conceived son Horus became the blueprint for our modern images of the Virgin Mary nursing Baby Jesus. And virtually all the elements of the Catholic ritual — the miter, the altar, the doxology, and communion, the act of " God-eating " — were taken directly from earlier pagan mystery religions."

Teabing groaned. "Don't get a symbologist started on Christian icons. Nothing in Christianity is original. The pre-Christian God Mithras — called the Son of God and the Light of the World — was born on December 25, died, was buried in a rock tomb, and then resurrected in three days. By the way, December 25 is also the birthday of

Osiris (an Egyptian god, usually identified as the god of the afterlife, the underworld and the dead), Adonis (a youth of remarkable beauty, the favourite of the goddess Aphrodite in Greek mythology, the god of beauty and desire), and Dionysus (the god of wine and fertility). The newborn Krishna (one of the most important of the Hindu gods) was presented with gold, frankincense, and myrrh. Even Christianity's weekly holy day was stolen from the pagans."

"What do you mean?"

"Originally," Langdon said, "Christianity honored the Jewish Sabbath of Saturday, but Constantine shifted it to coincide with the pagan's veneration day of the sun." He paused, grinning. "To this day, most churchgoers attend services on Sunday morning with no idea that they are there on account of the pagan sun god's weekly tribute — Sunday."

Sophie's head was spinning. "And all of this relates to the Grail?"

"Indeed," Teabing said. "Stay with me. During this fusion of religions, Constantine needed to strengthen the new Christian tradition, and held a famous ecumenical gathering known as the Council of Nicaea."

Sophie had heard of it only insofar as its being the birthplace of the Nicene Creed.

"At this gathering," Teabing said, "many aspects of Christianity were debated and voted upon — the date of Easter, the role of the bishops, the administration of sacraments, and, of course, the divinity of Jesus."

"I don't follow. His divinity?"

"My dear," Teabing declared, "until that moment in history, Jesus was viewed by His followers as a mortal prophet... a great and powerful man, but a man nonetheless. A mortal."

"Not the Son of God?"

"Right," Teabing said. "Jesus' establishment as 'the Son of God' was officially proposed and voted on by the Council of Nicaea."

"Hold on. You're saying Jesus' divinity was the result of a vote?"

"A relatively close vote at that," Teabing added. "Nonetheless, establishing Christ's divinity was critical to the further unification of the Roman empire and to the new Vatican power base. By officially endorsing Jesus as the Son of God, Constantine turned Jesus into a deity who existed beyond the scope of the human world, an entity whose power was unchallengeable. This not only precluded further pagan challenges to Christianity, but now the followers of Christ were able to redeem themselves only via the established sacred channel — the Roman Catholic Church."

Sophie glanced at Langdon, and he gave her a soft nod of concurrence.

"It was all about power," Teabing continued. "Christ as Messiah was critical to the functioning of Church and state. Many scholars claim that the early Church literally stole Jesus from His original followers, hijacking His human message, shrouding it in an impenetrable cloak of divinity, and using it to expand their own power. I've written several books on the topic."

"And I assume devout Christians send you hate mail on a daily basis?"

"Why would they?" Teabing countered. "The vast majority of educated Christians know the history of their faith. Jesus was indeed a great and powerful man. Constantine's underhanded political maneuvers don't diminish the majesty of Christ's life. Nobody is saying Christ was a fraud, or denying that He walked the earth and inspired millions to better lives. All we are saying is that Constantine took advantage of Christ's substantial influence and importance. And in doing so, he shaped the face of Christianity as we know it today."

Sophie glanced at the art book before her, eager to move on and see the Da Vinci painting of the Holy Grail.

"The twist is this," Teabing said, talking faster now. "Because Constantine upgraded Jesus' status almost four centuries after Jesus' death, thousands of documents already existed chronicling His life as a mortal man. To rewrite the history books, Constantine knew he would need a bold stroke. From this sprang the most profound moment in Christian history." Teabing paused, eyeing Sophie. "Constantine commissioned and financed a new *Bible*, which omitted those gospels that spoke of Christ's human traits and embellished those gospels that made Him godlike. The earlier gospels were outlawed, gathered up, and burned."

"An interesting note," Langdon added. "Anyone who chose the forbidden gospels over Constantine's version was deemed a heretic. The word heretic derives from that moment in history. The Latin word haereticus means 'choice.' Those who 'chose' the original history of Christ were the world's first heretics."

"Fortunately for historians," Teabing said, "some of the gospels that Constantine attempted to eradicate managed to survive. *The Dead Sea Scrolls* were found in the 1950s hidden in a cave near Qumran in the Judean desert. And, of course, the *Coptic Scrolls* in 1945 at Nag Hammadi. In addition to telling the true Grail story, these documents speak of Christ's ministry in very human terms. Of course, the Vatican, in keeping with their tradition of misinformation, tried very hard to suppress the release of these scrolls. And why wouldn't they? The scrolls highlight glaring historical discrepancies and fabrications, clearly confirming that the modern *Bible* was compiled and edited by men who possessed a political agenda — to promote the divinity of the man Jesus Christ and use His influence to solidify their own power base."

"And yet," Langdon countered, "it's important to remember that the modern Church's desire to suppress these documents comes from a sincere belief in their established view of Christ. The Vatican is made up of deeply pious men who truly believe these contrary documents could only be false testimony."

Teabing chuckled as he eased himself into a chair opposite Sophie. "As you can see, our professor has a far softer heart for Rome than I do. Nonetheless, he is correct about the modern clergy believing these opposing documents are false testimony. That's understandable. Constantine's *Bible* has been their truth for ages. Nobody is more indoctrinated than the indoctrinator."

"What he means," Langdon said, "is that we worship the gods of our fathers."

"What I mean," Teabing countered, "is that almost everything our fathers taught us about Christ is false. As are the stories about the Holy Grail."

Sophie looked again at the Da Vinci quote before her. Blinding ignorance does mislead us. O! Wretched mortals, open your eyes!

I. **Read the passage above and decide whether the statement is true (T) or false (F).**

_____ 1. The real gospels have been destroyed because of wars between Christians and pagans.

_____ 2. The *Bible* was written for people to record history.

_____ 3. Jesus was Son of God because more voters on the Council of Nicaea thought so.

_____ 4. Constantine was once a very good businessman.

_____ 5. Da Vinci's opinions on the *Bible* are directly related to the Holy Grail.

_____ 6. All the elements of the Catholic ritual were taken directly from earlier pagan mystery religions.

_____ 7. The confirmation of Christ's divinity was important for Constantine to become more powerful.

_____ 8. Virgin Mary was actually Isis who nursed her son Horus.

II. Group discussion.

1. Teabing said in the text that " The Bible is a product of man, my dear. Not of God", so, do you agree with it? And why?
   _____
   _____
   _____

2. Have you ever read *The Da Vinci Code*? How truthful do you think it is? Please share your opinions with your classmates.
   _____
   _____
   _____

Unit 6
Religious Art

What do we mean when we speak of religious art? Do we mean that religious themes are depicted in the art? Do we mean that religious persons were the artists? Do we mean that some special religious group or church has decided that the art is orthodox and therefore official?

All of these definitions have been used at one time or another to define religious art. The most common definition is that religious art is that which depicts biblical themes. Such art abounds, particularly that done in earlier centuries; but it is still prominent today. The next suggestion — that art is what religious artists do — saw its highest expression in the Renaissance when the church employed great artists who experimented with themes not only from biblical settings but from classical mythology as well. Often in history, "religious art" was what the church officially declared to be religious art. The most extreme example of this style is to be recalled in the Inquisition of the sixteenth century and in iconoclastic excesses right up to the present time.

Now the fact is that the very expression, religious art, is problematic. Biblical themes may be used in a painting but for irreligious purposes. The religion of the artist is ultimately irrelevant to the quality of his work, so that "faithful" painters may not be any more successful in doing "religious" art than nonbelievers. Some of the most powerful "religious art" of recent times has been done by artists professedly skeptical of the values of religious traditions.

It may well be that the interest that church folk show in defining religious art is but an example of the bad religious habit of the church to divide the religious from the secular, the O. K. and the not O. K, the clean and the impure. Such an attitude is contrary to the highest sense of the Christian view of the world and history and the intention of the gospel. God speaks to the world through its fullness and its roughness as well as from its particularity and its religious traditions.

What do we mean by the word religion? It comes from an ancient Latin word that means simply "to tie things together." Religion is the human quest for coherence and meaning in the understanding of the world. When the most primitive cultures first sought to see some connection between birth and death and the seasons of the year, they were constructing a religious view. When various forms of idolatry became part of their effort to influence the world, they were merely trying to tie all things together, to make sense out of a world that often proved hostile to human feelings. Religion is the generic word for Christianity. It is not synonymous with Christianity. Christianity is a form of religion, although to many of us it is the highest form. Religion is whatever posture is taken toward the world and its events and power that seek to tie all things together into a coherent and experiential whole.

Now it is easy to see where all the trouble in the definition of the term "religious art" arises. According to the above argument, art does not have to have biblical subject matter to be "religious." Any felt passion or insight about the world, expressed with power, ought to be considered religious art. In fact, we know that in earlier cultures, religion and art were almost the same thing. The religious buildings, icons, and music of a culture are art; and its art is its religion.

"Art" is the process of expressing in concrete form or event human emotions and aspirations, ranging from the simple joys of being to complex philosophical expression. A work of art is a concrete thing, an event that helps the participant to bridge his experience with that of the artist or the group or the religious values expressed therein. If one accepts this definition, there is no such thing as "art"; there are only the things we make to tell our stories as human beings with religious purposes. Sister Corita Kent, the famous pop artist, once said in a poster, "We have no art here. We only do the best we can."

Somewhere we received the idea that art must be pretty or polished or symmetrical or restful. It may express those possibilities. But, if our definition is correct, it must also at times be ugly, rough, asymmetrical, and jarring. Why? Because men and women sense their world that way some of the time — maybe most of the time.

How then are we to judge whether a work of art is a good piece of art or whether it is religious art? The answer is that this is probably an irrelevant question. The most important question is this: Is the work of art expressive of a powerful view of life and, regardless of subject matter, does it stir some religious sensitivity in the viewer?

The late Paul Tillich, a great Christian theologian, suggested that a work of art could have religious subject matter and still be an irreligious statement. On the other hand, a work of art on a non-biblical subject could be expressed with such power that it would be a profoundly religious painting. These statements may seem contradictory to you. But let us look at them carefully.

Tillich believed that just stating a religious theme was not adequate. A religious painting of this type would seem to carry the entire religious message. The experience of the viewer would be limited to his knowledge of the particular religious scene. On the other hand, a treatment of a common event in human life and experience, so touched by human sense that its power still grips the viewer, is unmistakably a "religious" event. It ties things together.

Look at the painting of Holman Hunt's *The Light of the World*. It is pretty. It expresses a fine personal sentiment. It is full of rich symbols. It contains religious subject matter. But it falls short of being a powerful statement of human emotion or aspiration. Now look at the painting of Georges Rouault's *Old King*. It shows a powerful monarch who sits with a frail flower in his hand, his jaw tight, as he contemplates the finality of life and the emptiness of temporal power. Which painting is more religious? They are both "religious," but only Rouault's is also great art.

Let us now check our theory by looking at two artistic statements about Jesus. Look at the widely loved *Head of Christ* by Warner Sallman; and then consider the head of Christ by Matthias Grunewald from the Isenheim altarpiece in Germany. Sallman's Christ is theatrical, handsome, European, blond. The full emotional weight of the painting is carried in the flaccid expression and the uplifted eyes. The face is that of a slightly effeminate and untroubled person. In short, it is our culture's expression of confidence in a less than powerful, prophetic, and effective Lord. Grunewald, on the other hand, depicts Christ in suffering on the cross. A frightful expression of shock and pain is the dominant theme. The skin of our Lord is bleeding, and the crown of thorns is pressed down to draw blood. By superficial standards this is an "ugly" Christ.

The question we must now ask is this: Which of these depictions of our Lord speaks more nearly to our sense of the power and mystery of God's mighty act of Incarnation? Is it the calm, cool, and effeminate Lord, or is it the victim — the one who took into himself the suffering of the world to reveal God's love? Modern people may want to like Sallman's Christ, but the tragic events of our time make the sixteenth-century Christ of Grunewald more powerful. We can identify with this Christ.

This insight brings us to the final problem in our discussion of religious art. Art is so important in the life of man and society that from the beginning of civilization tyrants have tried to control it. Keep the horizons of art no wider than the expectations of the rulers and you have kept a people under control. That is why the Nazis in Germany and the Communists in Russia have caused artists much trouble. That is why any attack on the artist in our culture is ultimately an attack on our own freedom to know and believe.

Even Plato suggested that in his *Perfect Republic* the artists ought to be rigorously controlled. We live in a free society; and if artists are free, they can be prophets in that society. They tell us what we may not have the imagination to see and think. They tell us secrets of our own hearts which religious traditions may not permit us to confess. In short they perform a kind of religious task for us all. They keep us open to the spirit of newness and innovation in the quest for meaning in human history and life. Without them, life would be merely the dull routine of what is apparent and not real, what is accustomed and not novel, what is required and not daring.

If you have not been to the local gallery in your museum or at the college or university near you, why not go soon and ask yourself some of the questions posed in this essay? Get acquainted with an artist and find out what makes him or her think and speak. Then, in your own reflection on the meaning of life, ask yourself this question: How do I tie it all together?

Religion is life, and the life that is lived without questions and spiritual wrestling is really a dull life indeed. When our minds and religious senses become dull and corrupt, then the glory of God and the blazing intentions of our Lord for our lives are unable to register in our daily existence. That is why religion and art are part of the wider quest for meaning. That is why we need them both.

(Text source: *Loving God with One's Mind*, by F. Thomas Trotter, 1987.)

Section A: Text-based Reading Comprehension

I. Choose the best answer according to the passage.
1. Which one of the following can be called both religious and great art?
   A. Holman Hunt's *The Light of the World*
   B. Georges Rouault's *Old King*
   C. Warner Sallman's *Head of Christ*
   D. Plato's *Perfect Republic*
2. According to Plato, artists are allowed to do the following except _____.
   A. to predict future

B. to give us imagination to see and think
   C. to tell us secrets of our hearts
   D. to open our spirit of peculiar things
3. The word "religion" in the text can mean the following except _____.
   A. the quest for coherence and meaning of the world
   B. the genetic word for Christianity
   C. a synonym of Christianity
   D. to tie things together
4. Which one is in conformity with the author's opinion?
   A. Artistic works are about concrete things.
   B. Art must be pretty, symmetrical or restful.
   C. A religious event should be a common event in human life.
   D. We need religion and art both in our life.
5. Which one of the following statements is false?
   A. Art is the process of expressing in concrete form.
   B. Art might be something pretty or polished or symmetrical or restful.
   C. Art may not exist at all according to the author.
   D. Art can be rarely understood by ordinary beings.

II. Answer the following questions.
1. What is the relationship between art and religion according to the author?

2. What are the examples used in explaining the connotation of "art" in the text?

III. Further discussion.
1. How is religious art defined in the text? Give three examples of religious art in your own culture.

2. What are the roles and functions that art performs in modern life?

Section B: Vocabulary

I. Fill in the blanks with the proper forms of the words given below.

depict	inquisition	secular	coherence	grip
polish	effeminate	flaccid	dominant	rigorous
innovation	wrestle	idolatry	quest	confess

1. An overall theme will help to give your essay _____.
2. Even while the muscles appear _____, some nerve threads may be functional.
3. The arms trade should be subject to _____ controls.
4. Children's books often _____ farmyard animals as gentle, lovable creatures.
5. The company can't preserve it _____ position in the market.
6. Their affection for her soon increased almost to _____.
7. Our directors took time out from their own recession problems to _____ with our worries.
8. You must take a _____ on yourself and do your lessons now.
9. The East, abandoning its _____ magnificence was descending into a valley.
10. The vegetarian burger was a(n) _____ which was rapidly exported to Britain.
11. It was Christmas, so Ellen gave the dining room a little extra spit and _____.
12. Contrary to his _____ appearance, he said without reserve during interview.
13. I was subjected to a lengthy _____ into the state of my marriage and the size of my bank balance.
14. She went to India on a spiritual _____.
15. I found it all confusing, I must _____.

II. Root and word formation.

1. Study the following roots and list more examples in the space provided.

Root	Meaning	Examples	More examples
-prehend (prehens)	to take, to seize	apprehend, prehensile	
-prob (prov)	to test, to try, to examine, good, proper	probe, improve	
-quest	to ask, to seek	bequest, inquest	
-rupt	to break	interrupt, disrupt	

Unit 6 Religious Art   91

B. Fill in the blanks with the proper forms of the words given below.

| apprehensive | probe | abrupt | request |
| comprehensible | improve | corrupt | bequest |

1. She tried to _____ my mind and discover what I was thinking.
2. You often find a writer's books more _____ if you know about his life.
3. I bought it at the _____ of my father.
4. Our detergent now has a new _____ formula.
5. He looked _____ as he waited for the result to be broadcast.
6. She was sent to prison for trying to _____ a policeman.
7. The train came to a(n) _____ stop, making many passengers fall of their steps.
8. He made the library a(n) _____ of 50,000 pounds.

Section C: Cloze

Fill in the blanks with the proper forms of the words given below.

| over | at | on | away | what |
| up | whose | grow | by | though |

I would have given much to have possessed the art of sketching, for many of the faces became wonderfully interesting when unconscious. Some grew stern and grim, the men evidently dreaming of war, as they gave orders, groaned __1__ their wounds, or damned the rebels vigorously; some __2__ sad and infinitely pathetic, as if the pain borne silently all day, revenged itself by now betraying what the man's pride had concealed so well. Often the roughest grew young and pleasant when sleep smoothed the hard lines away, letting the real nature assert itself; many almost seemed to speak, and I learned to know these men better __3__ night than through any intercourse by day. Sometimes they disappointed me, for faces that looked merry and good in the light, grew bad and sly when the shadows came; and __4__ they made no confidences in words, I read their lives, leaving them to wonder __5__ the change of manner this midnight magic wrought in their nurse. A few talked busily; one drummer boy sang sweetly, though no persuasions could win a note from him by day; and several depended on being told __6__ they had talked of in the morning. Even my constitutionals in the chilly halls, possessed a certain charm, for the house was never still. Sentinels tramped round it all night long, their muskets glittering in the wintry moonlight as they walked, or stood before the doors, straight and silent, as figures of stone, causing one to conjure __7__ romantic visions of guarded forts, sudden surprises, and daring deeds; for in these war times the hum drum life of Yankeedom had vanished, and the most prosaic feel some thrill of that excitement which stirs the nation's heart, and makes its capital a camp of hospitals. Wandering up and down these lower halls, I often heard cries from above, steps hurrying to and fro, saw surgeons passing up, or men coming down carrying a stretcher, where lay a long white figure, __8__ face was shrouded and whose fight was done. Sometimes I stopped to watch the passers in the street, the moonlight shining __9__ the spire opposite, or the gleam of some vessel floating, like a white-winged sea-gull, down the broad Potomac, whose fullest flow can never wash __10__ the red stain of the land.

Section D: Reading Skills Training

Directions: The following exercises are meant to improve your fast reading ability. And you are suggested to go over the passages quickly and then answer all the questions within 25 minutes.

Passage 1
For questions 1 -7, please mark
    Y (for YES) if the statement agrees with the information given in the passage;
    N (for NO) if the statement contradicts the information given in the passage;
    NG (for NOT GIVEN) if the statement is not given in the passage.

For questions 8 -10, complete the sentences with the information given in the passage.

1. _____ Like a radial tire, the area just under the shark's collagen "radials" is inflated by air pressure too.
2. _____ Normally when a fish or other object moves quickly through the water, a laminar flow can be formed when the water flows turbulent past the body of the dolphin.
3. _____ For most animals, their movement or locomotion can be used to find food, escape enemies, find food and explore new living places.
4. _____ The muscle is the key to the shark's impressive quick speed of locomotion on its prey.
5. _____ Unlike humans, movement for animals needs a long natural evolution through millions of years.
6. _____ Travelling the same distance, a slug consumes much less energy than a mouse does.
7. _____ The Duke University biologists discovered that the shark stretches its collagen fibers greatly when bending its body in swimming.
8. Collagen fibers can either store or release large amounts of energy depending on whether the fibers are _____.
9. When the shark detects _____, some fantastic involuntary changes take place.

10. Due to their inefficient use of energy, the slugs are forced to confine themselves to small areas for obtaining food and _____.

Animals on the Move

It looked like a scene from "Jaws" but without the dramatic music. A huge shark was lowly swimming through the water, its tail swinging back and forth like the pendulum of a clock.

Suddenly sensitive nerve ending in the shark's skin picked up vibrations of a struggling fish. The shark was immediately transformed into a deadly, efficient machine of death. With muscles taut, the shark knifed through the water at a rapid speed. In a flash the shark caught its victim, a large fish, in its powerful jaws. Then, jerking its head back and forth, the shark tore huge chunks of flesh from its victim and swallowed them. Soon the action was over.

Moving to Survive

In pursuing its prey, the shark demonstrated in a dramatic way the important role of movement, or locomotion, in animals.

Like the shark, most animals use movement to find food. They also use locomotion to escape enemies, find a mate, and explore new territories. The methods of locomotion include crawling, hopping, slithering, flying, swimming, or walking.

Humans have the added advantage of using their various inventions to move about in just about any kind of environment. Automobiles, rockets, and submarines transport humans from deep oceans to as far away as the moon. However, for other animals movement came about naturally through millions of years of evolution. One of the most successful examples of animal locomotion is that of the shark. Its ability to quickly zero in on its prey has always impressed scientists. But it took a detailed study by Duke University marine biologists S. A. Wainwright, F. Vosburgh, and J. H. Hebrank to find out how the sharks did it. In their study the scientists observed sharks swimming in a tank at Marine land in Saint Augustine, Fla. Movies were taken of the sharks' movements and analyzed. Studies were also made of shark skin and muscle.

Skin Is the Key

The biologists discovered that the skin of the shark is the key to the animal's high efficiency in swimming through the water. The skin contains many fibers that crisscross like the inside of a belted radial tire. The fibers are called collagen fibers. These fibers can either store or release large amounts of energy depending on whether the fibers are relaxed or taut. When the fibers are stretched, energy is stored in them the way energy is stored in the string of a bow when pulled tight. When the energy is released, the fibers become relaxed.

The Duke University biologists have found that the greatest stretching occurs where the shark bends its body while swimming. During the body's back and forth motion, fibers along the outside part of the bending body stretch greatly. Much potential energy is stored in the fibers. This energy is released when the shark's body snaps back the other way.

As energy is alternately stored and released on both sides of the animal's body, the tail whips strongly back and forth. This whip-like action propels the animal through the water like a living bullet.

Source of Energy

What causes the fibers to store so much energy? In finding the answer the Duke University scientists learned that the shark's similarity to a belted radial tire doesn't stop with the skin. Just as a radial tire is inflated by pressure, so, too, is the area just under the shark's collagen "radials". Instead of air pressure, however, the pressure in the shark may be due to the force of the blood pressing on the collagen fibers.

When the shark swims slowly, the pressure on the fibers is relatively low. The fibers are more relaxed, and the shark is able to bend its body at sharp angles. The animal swims this way when looking around for food or just swimming. However, when the shark detects an important food source, some fantastic involuntary changes take place.

The pressure inside the animal may increase by 10 times. This pressure change greatly stretches the fibers, enabling much energy to be stored. This energy is then transferred to the tail, and the shark is off. The rest of the story is predictable.

Dolphin Has Speed Record

Another fast marine animal is the dolphin. This seagoing mammal has been clocked at speeds of 32 kilometers (20 miles) an hour. Biologists studying the dolphin have discovered that, like the shark, the animal's efficient locomotion can be traced to its skin. A dolphin's skin is made up in such a way that it offers very little resistance to the water flowing over it. Normally when a fish or other object moves slowly through the water, the water flows smoothly past the body. This smooth flow is known as laminar flow. However, at faster speeds the water becomes more turbulent along the moving fish. This turbulence muses friction and slows the fish down.

In a dolphin the skin is so flexible that it bends and yields to the waviness of the water. The waves, in effect, become tucked into the skin's folds. This allows the rest of the water to move smoothly by in a laminar flow. Where other animals would be slowed by turbulent water at rapid speeds, the dolphin can race through the water at record breaking speeds.

Other Animals Less Efficient

Not all animals move as efficiently as sharks and dolphins. Perhaps the greatest loser in locomotion efficiency is the slug. The slug, which looks like a snail without a shell, lays down a slimy trail over which it crawls. It uses so much energy producing the slimy mucus and crawling over it that a mouse traveling the same distance uses only one twelfth as much energy.

Scientists say that because of the slug's inefficient use of energy, its lifestyle must be restricted. That is, the animals are forced to confine themselves to small areas for obtaining food and finding proper living conditions. Have humans ever been faced with this kind of problem?

Passage 2

The central tenet of Christianity is the belief in Jesus as the Son of God and the Messiah (Christ). Christians believe that Jesus, as the Messiah, was anointed by God as savior of humanity, and hold that Jesus' coming was the fulfillment of messianic prophecies of the Old Testament. The Christian concept of the Messiah differs significantly from the contemporary Jewish concept. The core Christian belief is that through belief in and acceptance of the death and resurrection of Jesus, sinful humans can be reconciled to God and thereby are offered salvation and the promise of eternal life.

While there have been many theological disputes over the nature of Jesus over the earliest centuries of Christian history, Christians generally believe that Jesus is God incarnate and " true God and true man" (or both fully divine and fully human). Jesus, having become fully human, suffered the pains and temptations of a mortal man, but did not sin. As fully God, he rose to life again. According to the Bible, " God raised him from the dead", he ascended to heaven, is " seated at the right hand of the Father" and will ultimately return to fulfill the rest of Messianic prophecy such as the Resurrection of the dead, the Last Judgment and final establishment of the Kingdom of God.

According to the canonical gospels of Matthew and Luke, Jesus was conceived by the Holy Spirit and born from the Virgin Mary. Little of Jesus' childhood is recorded in the canonical Gospels, however infancy Gospels were popular in antiquity. In comparison, his adulthood, especially the week before his death, is well documented in the Gospels contained within the New Testament. The Biblical accounts of Jesus' ministry include: his baptism, miracles, preaching, teaching, and deeds.

Read the passage above and answer the following questions.
11. In Christianity, Jesus is considered both as _____ and _____.
12. Christians believe that Jesus comes to this world to _____.
13. Which of the following is correct based on this passage?
    A. Christians believe that Jesus is a fully man.
    B. Jesus' childhood is recorded in the canonical Gospels.
    C. Jesus' adulthood is well recorded in the Gospels.

D. Christians believe that all sinful humans can be offered salvation and the promise of eternal life.

Passage 3

The 66 chapters of Isaiah consist primarily of prophecies of the judgments awaiting nations that are persecuting Judah. These nations include Babylon, Assyria, Philistia, Moab, Syria, Israel (the northern kingdom), Ethiopia, Egypt, Arabia, and Phoenicia. The prophecies concerning them can be summarized as saying that Jehovah is the God of the whole earth, and that nations which think of themselves as secure in their own power might well be conquered by other nations, at God's command.

Chapter 6 describes Isaiah's call to be a prophet of God. Chapters 35 – 39 provide material about King Hezekiah. Chapters 24 – 34, while too complex to characterize easily, are primarily concerned with prophecies of a messiah, the Lord's "chosen one", a person anointed or given power by God, and of the messiah's kingdom, where justice and righteousness will reign. This section is seen by Jews as describing a king, a descendant of their great king, David, who will make Judah a great kingdom and Jerusalem a truly holy city.

The prophecy continues with what can be characterized as a "book of comfort" which begins in chapter 40 and completes the writing. In the first eight chapters of this book of comfort, Isaiah prophesies the deliverance of the Jews from the hands of the Babylonians and restoration of Israel as a unified nation in the land promised to them by God. Isaiah reaffirms that the Jews are indeed the chosen people of God in chapter 44 and that Jehovah is the only God for the Jews as he will show his power over the gods of Babylon in due time in chapter 46. In chapter 45: 1 the Persian ruler Cyrus is named as the messiah who will overthrow the Babylonians and allow the return of Israel to their original land. The remaining chapters of the book contain prophecies of the future glory of Zion under the rule of a righteous servant (52 and 54). Chapter 53 contains a poetic prophecy about this servant which is generally considered by Christians to refer to Jesus, although Jews generally interpret it as a reference to God's people. Although there is still the mention of judgment of false worshippers and idolaters (65 & 66), the book ends with a message of hope of a righteous ruler who extends salvation to his righteous subjects living in the Lord's kingdom on earth.

Read the passage above and answer the following questions.

14. The prophecies of judgments can be summarized as _____.
15. The book ends with _____.

Further Reading

Religion and Language

A religion instinct

In *Religion as Narrative*, I put forward the view that the basis of religion is not belief but is narrative. Now, narrative is largely a matter of language: narratives are primarily expressed in words (also in pictures, but the pictures generally require verbal elaboration if they are to be understood).

There is thus a trivial sense in which religion and language are related to each other. It would be impossible to acquire a religion without the medium of language. However, I want to suggest that the connection is deeper than this, and that both religion and language may be closely connected at a deep level and may be acquired in quite similar ways.

What needs to be explained about religion?

Two aspects of religion require explanation. First, it is seemingly universal in all human societies. Second, although religions may vary greatly from one society to another, they possess certain features in common that make us able to identify them as religions. We know a religion when we meet it.

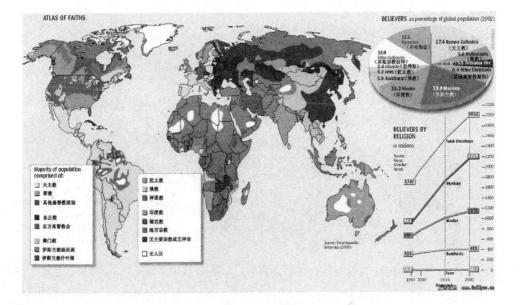

Is there a "deep structure" for religion?

Many people have interpreted this universality and similarity as indicating the presence of a "religion instinct", an inbuilt tendency to religious belief and practice in all human beings. Some have even speculated that there are brain structures that give rise to this. Now, very similar arguments have been applied to language.

Every human society we have encountered has possessed language, and Noam Chomsky has famously claimed that there are similarities in the structure of all languages that point to the existence of a "Universal Grammar" (Chomsky 1972). The grammar or "deep structure" of human languages is very complex, yet young children seem to have an innate ability to master this complexity within a short time, as if by instinct. This has suggested to many people that the rules of grammar are in some sense built into the human brain during evolution.

If this idea is correct, might not the same be true of religion? Religion, after all, is apparently a near-universal in human societies, like language, so perhaps there is a "deep structure" for religion just as there seems to be for language.

Language and religion as mind parasites

I want to take up this idea but to modify it in what I hope is a constructive way. In his book *The Symbolic Species* Terrence Deacon rejects Chomsky's view and proposes instead the hypothesis that languages evolve in a kind of symbiotic relation with the human mind (Deacon, 1997). The fact that young children are able to learn languages with apparent ease, he suggests, does not mean that they have some extraordinary innate linguistic ability but rather that human languages have evolved to be learned easily by immature minds.

There is a two-fold evolution going on here: certainly the human brain has evolved linguistic capabilities that are absent in the brains of other primates, but at the same time languages have adapted themselves to be readily learnable. This clearly has something in common with Dawkins's meme idea, which Deacon does mention in passing, but it places more emphasis on evolutionary change in language than we find in the writings of most memeticists.

Resemblances between language and religion

If we now look at religion we find, I believe, a number of rather close similarities with Deacon's view of language. I want to suggest that religion, like language, has evolved to be easily learned by children. The following features seem to be relevant.

1. Religion and children

Religious people are often reproved by the non-religious, and even by some co-religionists, for having a "childish" view of God; and this is in a sense reflected in references to God the Father (today often transformed by feminists into God the Mother). If religion has evolved to be easily learned by children, this makes good sense. Is this perhaps what Jesus meant when he said "Except ye be converted, and become as little children, ye shall not enter into the kingdom of heaven." (Matthew 18, 3)?

2. Conversion vs. early-acquired religion

The language-learning ability of children is different from that of adults. There is a long-held view that this indicates a "critical period" for language learning, similar to the "imprinting" phenomenon in birds. Deacon disagrees, suggesting instead that a degree of immaturity may be actually necessary for language acquisition in this way.

Whatever the explanation, the phenomenon certainly exists, as anyone who has tried to learn a new language in later life can testify. But religion is acquired by children in a very similar way to language. Many people are taught religion literally at their mothers' knees, and religions infused early in life in this way have a different "feel" from those that may be adopted later as the result of conversion.

Religious beliefs inculcated in childhood are also difficult to shake off, just as one's "mother tongue" is more persistent in the face of disuse than languages learned in later life. Seen in this way, the well-known if apocryphal Jesuit saying "Give me a boy until he's seven and he's mine for life" takes on a new significance.

3. The language of religion

Acquiring a religion involves to some extent learning a new vocabulary and syntax: for example, the old Quaker use of "thee" and, in some Christian circles, phraseology such as "believing 'on' Jesus" instead of the vernacular "believing 'in'". And because what is said may partially condition what can be thought, the use of such speech patterns will have subtle psychological effects on the speakers, tending to limit what can be named and hence what can be thought. Hence religion and language are closely connected at the structural level.

4. Sacred languages

Many religions have a sacred language (Hebrew for Judaism, classical Arabic for Islam, Sanskrit for Hinduism, Pali for Theravada Buddhism). Because religions are generally ancient the languages they use are often partially or wholly unintelligible to the laity and sometimes even the clergy, but contrary to what religious modernizers suppose, this linguistic remoteness is a strength, not a weakness.

Misguided attempts to bring the language up to date often coincide with a loss of religious faith, and it is difficult to say what is cause and what is effect. Many Roman Catholics still lament the abandonment of the Latin Mass in favour of the vernacular, and disuse of the Book of Common Prayer by the Church of England has not prompted an influx of young worshippers to the pews.

5. Universal features of religion?

The grammatical similarities among languages find a parallel in religions. For example, there seems to be a tendency for two separate tendencies to form within mature religions. In Christianity we have Catholicism and Protestantism: Catholicism goes in for devotion to the Virgin Mary and the saints and produces complex vestments and rituals, all of which are frowned on to a greater or lesser extent by Protestants. In Buddhism there is the distinction between Theravada and Mahayana: the Theravada is relatively austere and unemotional, whereas the Mahayana has the Bodhisattvas (who compare in some ways with the saints in Catholicism) and elaborate ceremonies.

Within Islam there are likewise differences in tone between Sunni and Shia: in a Shia country such as Iran you frequently see pictures of Ali, Hussain and other "saints" in taxis and elsewhere which are curiously reminiscent of Greek icons and Catholic saints' pictures. It would of course be wrong to push these resemblances too far, yet it is difficult not to notice the similarities in "feel". Catholicism, Mahayana, and Shiite Islam have something in common, and so do Protestantism, Theravada, and Sunni Islam.

6. Religions, like languages evolve

Languages, as Deacon emphasizes, are not static but evolve over time; they behave in fact like living organisms. The same is true of religions. Deacon writes: "As a language passes from generation to generation, the vocabulary and syntactical rules tend to get modified by transmission errors, by the active creativity of its users,

and by influences from other languages... Eventually words, phraseology and syntax will diverge so radically that people will find it impossible to mix elements of both without confusion. By analogy to biological evolution, different lineages of a common ancestral language will diverge so far from each other as to become reproductively incompatible. "

If we substitute "religion" for "language" we have a pretty exact description of how Christianity evolved from Judaism. They have become different species, which can no longer "interbreed". Within religions there are often subspecies — the different denominations within Christianity, for example.

7. Did language and religion originate together?

Finally, and very speculatively, may the origins of both language and religion go back to the very beginnings of modern human consciousness? Many people believe that there was a qualitative shift in human consciousness about 50,000 years ago — the so-called Great Leap Forward, when tool-making became more complex and the cave paintings in France and Spain first appeared. We do not know why these paintings were made but a prevalent idea is that they had some sort of religious or magical significance. We also do not know when language first developed, but again it is speculated that an elaborate form of speech first became possible to humans at about the same time as the paintings. If these ideas are at all correct, it would follow that language and religion were closely connected at their very inception.

Religion: parasite or symbiont?

According to Deacon, it is possible to think of languages as parasites or viruses. However, that is probably too severe, as he concedes, since languages are after all beneficial to their hosts and should therefore better be regarded as symbionts. So is religion a parasite or a symbiont? We could not do without language, but could we do without religion? Perhaps it has become so deeply infused into our minds and our culture that we cannot rid ourselves of it. It may be like the mitochondria in our cells; these were originally free-living organisms, but at some stage in the distant past they became permanent denizens of all "advanced" cells, which depend on them for their ability to use oxygen for energy. Have religions become our psychological mitochondria?

As we contemplate the spread of fundamentalism and fanaticism today among many religions, with all that this portends for continuing conflict and perhaps the disintegration of society, it is difficult to avoid a sense of helplessness. If it is true, as I suspect it may be, that religion is so deeply interfused in our mental make-up that most of us cannot do without it, our outlook may be bleak.

I. Read the passage above and decide whether the statement is true (T) or false (F).

_____ 1. Religion is universal in all human societies.

_____ 2. There exists a "critical period" for children to learn language, after which children may be harder to begin to learn.

_____ 3. The author thinks that religion is either beneficial or harmful to its host.

_____ 4. There's a "deep structure" for language as well as for religion.
_____ 5. Religion and language are closely related at the structural level.
_____ 6. There are some similarities in Catholicism and Theravada as well as Protestantism and Sunni Islam.
_____ 7. Without language, we can't learn religion.
_____ 8. The reason why language is easy for young children to learn is because languages have developed.

II. Research and mini-presentation:

Mark Vernon, a writer, teacher and psychotherapist, claimed in his famous book *Science, Religion and the Meaning of life* that from Newton and Descartes to Darwin and the discovery of the genome, religion has been pushed back further and further while science has gained ground. Do you agree with him or not? Do some researches in the library or on the Internet, and present your viewpoints to the class.

_____
_____
_____

Topic 3 Speech

A speech is a formal talk which someone gives to an audience. Therefore, it is frequently termed as Public Speaking (sometimes termed Oratory), which is the process and act of speaking or giving a lecture to a group of people in a structured, deliberate manner intended to inform, influence, or entertain a listening audience. Public speaking is commonly understood as face-to-face speaking between individuals and an audience for the purpose of communication. It is closely allied to "presenting", although the latter is more often associated with commercial activity. Most of the time, public speaking is to persuade the audience.

In public speaking, as in any form of communication, there are five basic elements, often expressed as "who is saying what to whom using what medium with what effects?" The purpose of public speaking can range from simply transmitting information, to motivating people to act, to simply telling a story. Good orators should be able to change the emotions of their listeners, not just inform them. Public speaking can also be considered a discourse community. Interpersonal communication and public speaking have several components that embrace such things as motivational speaking, leadership/personal development, business, customer service, large group communication, and mass communication. Public speaking can be a powerful tool to use for purposes such as motivation, influence, persuasion, informing, translation, or simply ethos.

Selected words on speech:

forensics	辩论术	progymnasmata	初级修辞训练
debate	辩论	extemporaneous	即兴的
rhetoric	修辞	oratory	演讲术
discourse	演讲	impromptu	即席的
orator	演说者	sophist	诡辩者

Unit 7
The Significance of Poetry

When I began to think of what I should say to you this evening, I wished only to express very simply my appreciation of the high honour which the Swedish Academy has thought fit to confer upon me. But to do this adequately proved no simple task: my business is with words, yet the words were beyond my command. Merely to indicate that I was aware of having received the highest international honour that can be bestowed upon a man of letters, would be only to say what everyone knows already. To profess my own unworthiness would be to cast doubt upon the wisdom of the Academy; to praise the Academy might suggest that I, as a literary critic, approved the recognition given to myself as a poet. May I  therefore ask that it be taken for granted, that I experienced, on learning of this award to myself, all the normal emotions of exaltation and vanity that any human being might be expected to feel at such a moment, with enjoyment of the flattery, and exasperation at the inconvenience, of being turned overnight into a public figure? Were the Nobel Award similar in kind to any other award, and merely higher in degree, I might still try to find words of appreciation: but since it is different in kind from any other, the expression of one's feelings calls for resources which language cannot supply.

I must therefore try to express myself in an indirect way, by putting before you my own interpretation of the significance of the Nobel Prize in Literature. If this were simply the recognition of merit, or of the fact that an author's reputation has passed the boundaries of his own country and his own language, we could say that hardly any one of us at any time is, more than others, worthy of being so distinguished. But I find in the Nobel Award something more and something different from such recognition. It seems to me more the election of an individual, chosen from time to time from one nation or another, and selected by something like an act of grace, to fill a peculiar role and to become a peculiar symbol. A ceremony takes place, by which a man is suddenly endowed with some function which he did not fill before. So the question is not whether he was worthy to be so singled out, but whether he can perform the function which you have assigned to him: the function of serving as a representative, so far as any man can be of thing of far greater importance than the value of what he himself has written.

Poetry is usually considered the most local of all the arts. Painting, sculpture, architecture, music, can be enjoyed by all who see or hear. But language, especially the language of poetry, is a different matter. Poetry, it might seem, separates peoples instead of uniting them.

But on the other hand we must remember that while language constitutes a barrier, poetry itself gives us a reason for trying to overcome the barrier. To enjoy poetry belonging to another language is to enjoy an understanding of the people to whom that language belongs, an understanding we can get in no other way. We may think also of the history of poetry in Europe, and of the great influence that the poetry of one language can exert on another; we must remember the immense debt of every considerable poet to poets of other languages than his own; we may reflect that the poetry of every country and every language would decline and perish, were it not nourished by poetry in foreign tongues. When a poet speaks to his own people, the voices of all the poets of other languages who have influenced him are speaking also. And at the same time he himself is speaking to younger poets of other languages, and these poets will convey something of his vision of life and something of the spirit of his people, to their own. Partly through his influence on other poets, partly through translation, which must be also a kind of recreation of his poems by other poets, partly through readers of his language who are not themselves poets, the poet can contribute toward understanding between peoples.

In the work of every poet there will certainly be much that can only appeal to those who inhabit the same region, or speak the same language, as the poet. But nevertheless there is a meaning to the phrase "the poetry of Europe", and even to the word "poetry" the world over. I think that in poetry people of different countries and different languages — though it be apparently only through a small minority in any one country — acquire an understanding of each other which, however partial, is still essential. And I take the award of the Nobel Prize in Literature, when it is given to a poet, to be primarily an assertion of the supra-national value of poetry. To make that affirmation, it is necessary from time to time to designate a poet: and I stand before you, not on my own merits, but as a symbol, for a time, of the significance of poetry.

(Thomas Stearns Eliot's speech at the Nobel Banquet at the City Hall in Stockholm, December 10, 1948.)

Section A: Text-based Reading Comprehension

I. Choose the best answer according to the passage.
1. The author said that to express his appreciation to the Swedish Academy was not a simple task because _____.
    A. he had cast doubt upon the wisdom of the Academy
    B. he thought that words were beyond his command to express the complicated feelings he has to the Swedish Academy
    C. he didn't know what he has to say
    D. he was literary critic not a poet
2. The significance of the Nobel Prize in Literature for the author is _____.
    A. a great honor
    B. a kind of recognition
    C. a symbol of the significance of poetry
    D. international reputation
3. How does poetry overcome language barrier?
    A. Poetry unites people.
    B. Poetry makes communication easier.
    C. Poetry is universal without boundaries.
    D. Poetry makes supra-national understanding possible.
4. What is the author's opinion on the value of poetry?
    A. To acquire an understanding of people from different cultures
    B. To convey emotion
    C. To achieve international recognition
    D. To be awarded
5. What does "partial" probably mean in the last paragraph?
    A. Regional   B. Limited   C. Prejudiced   D. Unfair

II. Answer the following questions.
1. Why does the author say that Nobel Prize for him is a symbol of the significance of poetry at the end of the text?

_____

_____

2. What are the functions of poetry from the the author's point of view?

___

___

___

III. Further discussion.
1. Poetry is supra-national, as is stated in the passage "When a poet speaks to his own people, the voices of all the poets of other languages who have influenced him are speaking also". To what extent do you agree or disagree?

___

___

2. Some people criticize that the selection and judgment of Noble Prize for Literature is not neutral and fair, which may be influenced by religious, political or economical factors. To what extent do you agree or disagree?

___

___

Section B: Vocabulary

I. Fill in the blanks with the proper forms of the words given below.

confer	bestow	profess	exaltation	vanity
exasperation	endow	barrier	nourish	designate
cast	inhabit	perish	assign	single

1. The Sahara Desert is a natural _____ between North and Central Africa.
2. The chairman has _____ Christina as his successor.
3. There is growing _____ within the government at the failure of these policies to reduce unemployment.
4. He wished to _____ great honors upon the hero.
5. Sabrina had none of the _____ so often associated with beautiful women.
6. The Queen _____ knighthoods on several distinguished men.
7. Most plants are _____ by water drawn up through their roots.
8. She _____ not to be interested in money.
9. The state of Michigan has _____ three institutes to do research for industry.
10. And for a moment he was filled with a sort of _____ .
11. Those remote islands are _____ only by birds.
12. Detectives have been unable to _____ a motive for the murder.

13. Jimmy was thrilled when the teacher _____ out his poem and asked him to read it out.
14. He believes that Europe must create closer ties or it will _____.
15. _____ out by his family, he was forced to fend for himself.

II. Root and word formation.

1. Study the following roots and list more examples in the space provided.

Root	Meaning	Examples	More examples
-tort (tor)	to twist	extort, retort	
-tra (tract)	to draw	detract, abstract, attract	
-tribut	to give, to pay	attribute, contribute	
-val (vail)	worth, strong	available, prevail	

B. Fill in the blanks with the proper forms of the words given below.

contribute	retort	extract	attribute
protract	tortuous	prevail	contract

1. Let's not _____ the debate any further.
2. He _____ that it was my entire fault.
3. Everybody _____ towards Jane's present when she left the office.
4. He _____ a promise from me that I'd come to the party.
5. My arms are tired from steering along this _____ mountain road.
6. Susan _____ her success to hard work.
7. Our shop has entered into a _____ with a clothing firm to buy 100 coats a week.
8. Can I _____ upon you to stay a little longer?

Section C: Cloze

Fill in the blanks with the proper forms of the words given below.

despite	as	uniquely	behaviors	genes
born	it		culture	change	identify

___1___ differences in how culture is conceptualized, anthropologists do agree on some things. Most of them agree that culture is a ___2___ human characteristic that must be learned. Each new generation of humans has to learn it all over again, for although the capacity for culture is grounded in their biology and physical natures, it is not something inherited through one's ___3___. Individuals are not born with ___4___; they have to learn it. Being ___5___ in America gives people rights of citizenship, but he or she must learn the beliefs and behaviors that makes and __6__ him or her as an American. An individual can be born in France but can become English by learning those beliefs and __7__ of English culture. The fact that culture must be learned also means that it must be taught, making __8__ a group and shared phenomenon. Whether one prefers such a term as education, socialization, or enculturation, or even a generic term such as culturation for the process, culture transmission and acquisition represent the means by which cultures are reproduced. Anthropologists also agree that cultures are always __9__, because environments are always changing. No culture today is the same __10__ it has always been.

Section D: Reading Skills Training

Directions: The following exercises are meant to improve your fast reading ability. And you are suggested to go over the passages quickly and then answer all the questions within 25 minutes.

Passage 1
For questions 1-7, please mark
　　Y (for YES) if the statement agrees with the information given in the passage;
　　N (for NO) if the statement contradicts the information given in the passage;
　　NG (for NOT GIVEN) if the statement is not given in the passage.
For questions 8-10, complete the sentences with the information given in the passage.

1. _____ Citron-Fink lost her home, her cousins and kids when Sandy struck upstate New York.
2. _____ President Obama spent significant time on the issue of climate change in his second Inaugural Address.
3. _____ HuffPost on Friday reported how extreme weather might become still more extreme totally due to global warming.
4. _____ Some environmentalists do not believe what Obama said in his second Inaugural Address about his policy on climate change.
5. _____ In a 2012 poll by the Yale Project on Climate Change Communication, 88 percent of respondents supported that the U.S. should work to reduce global warming without considering economic costs.
6. _____ According to the text, the Republican-controlled House will not help Obama reduce global warming.
7. _____ According to Daniel Kish, Obama will be a little more flexible to carry out "his anti-fossil fuel agenda" in his second term.

8. Maisano predicts that _____ and other renewables will be continually made a "major piece of his equation" by Obama.
9. According to Maisano, the success of renewable energy sources often _____.
10. In Daniel Souweine's opinion, if the U. S. devote to _____ in the country, it's just going to face more extreme climate changes.

State of the Union: Climate Change Plan, Green Energy on Environmentalists' Wish List

Ronnie Citron-Fink of upstate New York personally felt the effects of Hurricane Irene, her cousins in Long Island lost a home to Superstorm Sandy and her Boston-based kids just experienced the latest "hundred-year event" to strike the Northeast in recent years, a record-breaking windstorm called "Nemo."

"The political is personal," said Citron-Fink, of the nonprofit Mom's Clean Air Force. "Now is the time for Obama to address our climate change concerns," adding to that list childhood asthma and other conditions linked to pollution from the burning of fossil fuels.

Expectations are high among many environmentalists going into Tuesday night's State of the Union. President Barack Obama devoted significant time to the issue of climate change last month in his second Inaugural Address, whetting their appetites for more.

"We would hope to hear the president underscore the strong case for action he made in his address and lay out some vision for how to tackle the issue, both by reducing emissions and by strengthening our resilience to climate impacts," said Elliot Diringer, executive vice president at the nonpartisan Center for Climate and Energy Solutions.

But as many experts also note, such hopes should probably be tempered. Obama is constrained by a ticking clock and partisan politics. How he uses his limited time and political capital in his speech, they say, will determine how much of an airing their issues will get.

"The question is how much to activate your base, and how much to poke Congress in the eye, and how much to actually set up negotiations when you're going to have to give in down road to achieve compromise," said Frank Maisano, an energy strategist at the law firm Bracewell & Giuliani. "I think all of those will be at play."

Maisano added that the traditional timeframe of 45 to 55 minutes doesn't allow much time for "nitty gritty" details. He said he expects "broad strokes" on complicated climate and energy issues, including their relation to wild weather.

In addition to coming off the hottest year on record, with devastating wildfires and droughts that have left the Mississippi River nearly unnavigable, climate scientists have cast dire warnings as a result of recent storms such as Hurricane Sandy and last weekend's blizzard. HuffPost reported on Friday how such extremes might become still more extreme, due in part to global warming.

"For people to be blind and say that the climate has nothing to do with this is just insane," Dawn DeLuca of Occupy Sandy New Jersey told HuffPost, referencing the devastation Sandy left in October.

In the past, Obama has approached the topics of the climate and clean energy in the context of the economy, emphasizing the promise of green jobs. But investing his minutes in an honest, albeit grim forecast of global warming's consequences for extreme weather and public health may more effectively communicate the weight of the issue, say some experts. As the National Journal put it last week, "Obama doesn't have to sugarcoat things this time around."

During his second inaugural speech, Obama recast confronting climate change as a moral obligation to future generations. Some environmentalists suggest that argument even falls short.

"They keep talking about climate change as if it's just something in the future," said DeLuca. "The future is here. It's happening as we speak. We need to start seeing some positive action now."

The president may have increased support for such action from his constituents. In a September 2012 poll by the Yale Project on Climate Change Communication, 88 percent of respondents said the U. S. should work to reduce global warming, regardless of economic costs. The survey also found that Americans are in fact making the connection between extreme weather and climate change.

While Obama may not be able to count on help from a Republican-controlled House, experts and advocates suggested he can use his executive authority through the Environmental Protection Agency to implement tougher regulations on the fossil fuel industry, whether in the form of standards on new coal-fired power plants or economic incentives to cut emissions.

"He can use the tools already within his control to pressure energy markets to price carbon immediately, because we need immediate action to head off climate change," said Arno Harris, CEO of the solar company Recurrent Energy.

"Probably the most important thing that the president can do — and not just in the State of the Union — is to keep making the case," added Diringer. "We're long overdue for a sensible and sustained conversation about both the risks and the opportunities, and no one is better placed to lead that conversation than the president."

A large portion of that conversation revolves around the distribution of energy sources in Obama's "all of the above" energy strategy.

Daniel Kish, senior vice president of American Energy Alliance, told HuffPost in an emailed statement that Obama, now that he's in his second term, has a bit more "flexibility" to push forward with "his anti-fossil fuel agenda."

"If there's anything we've learned from the past four years, it's that a wide gulf exists between the president's rhetoric on affordable energy sources and his actions," he said. "Americans can expect more of the same during this year's State of the Union address."

Maisano said he foresees Obama continuing to make wind, solar and other renewables a "major piece of his equation."

"There are great renewable stories out there, such as wind projects in the upper Midwest. Unfortunately, those great successes often go quietly unnoticed and what you do see is Solyndra and other failures of the solar industry. You do see wind laying off people because of uncertainty," said Maisano. "Those few negative things often undercut the story on some of these clean energy objectives."

Natural gas will also remain a major player in Obama's mix, predicted Maisano.

Perhaps there are no two environmental or energy issues that are sparking more debate today than the fate of the Keystone XL pipeline and the proliferation of hydraulic fracturing for natural gas, also known as fracking. Although probably an unrealistic expectation at this point, some environmentalists would like to hear Obama say he'll do away with both — or at least hear him address both issues.

"I think the environmental movement is waiting to hear what, if anything, he says about Keystone XL," Bill McKibben, co-founder of environmental group 350.org, told HuffPost in an email. "It's the one and only thing that's brought people in large numbers into the streets in years."

"If we devote to more natural gas in this country, it's just going to take us more slowly off the climate cliff," added Daniel Souweine, campaign director for the grassroots organization Forecast the Facts.

Citron-Fink said that she'd love to see a greater push for clean energy. And until or unless fracking is better studied and its effects on public health identified, she added, Obama's strategy should focus on renewables and not natural gas.

"We don't want any more dirty energy," she said. "We don't want this future for our children. We are seeing the effects now."

Passage 2

Some philosophers distinguish between personal ethics and social ethics. Personal ethics is concerned with how one should behave in relation to oneself, and social ethics on how one should behave in relation to others. Some philosophers consider the questions of social ethics to be closely related to those of political and legal philosophy. A paramount questioning this regard is that of the justice of the social/political institutions, especially the law — the theory of justice. This theory is concerned with the nature of a just law, whether one has a moral obligation to obey a so-called unjust law, and whether law itself can be defined independently of morality. Another question here is whether morality can be legislated, an issue which arises in disputes over racial integration or segregation (for example apartheid) and over legal restrictions on sexual relations (for example, homosexuality) and abortion.

Personal ethics refers to the individual's perception of right or wrong, based upon the system of values he believes in. Such a perception is, however, more than merely a personal opinion, because an opinion does not constitute an ethic. If the perception of right and wrong is to be a personal ethic, there must be a reference to some outside standard or agent. That means a set of generally accepted values, accepted as authoritative and acknowledged by a number of people, which can serve as a set of principles for personal conduct. A public official must, in other words, base his perceptions of right and wrong upon a standard that is generally recognized as such. Decisions based on religious doctrine are good examples.

Personal ethics is a reflection of a person's character. Character is made up of those principles and values that give your life direction, meaning and depth. These constitute your inner sense of what is right and what is wrong, based not on laws or rules of conduct but on who you are. They include traits such as integrity, honesty, courage, fairness and generosity — which arise, from the hard choices we have to make in life. So wrong lies simply in doing wrong, and not in getting caught.

Sometimes the basic view of success in a political career shifts to what may be called a "personality ethic". For instance, political success became more a function of charm, skills and techniques that, at least on the surface, lubricate the process of political interaction. Rather than struggle with thorny issues of right and wrong, politicians turn to making things run smoothly. Some of that philosophy expresses itself in harmless but superficial maxim such as "Smiling wins more votes than frowning". Other ideas were clearly manipulative or even deceptive — faking an interest in possible supporters' personal well-being so that they will like you, for instance. With a value system based solely on skill and personality, one may see powerful politicians as heroes. But despite the admiration we feel for these achievers, we should not necessarily look upon them as heroes. While skill is certainly needed for success, it can never guarantee personal happiness and fulfillment. These come from developing character.

Choose the best answer according to the passage.
11. We can learn from the passage that personal ethics _____.
    A. refers to a personal opinion of right or wrong
    B. can be a reflection of a person's character

C. is the same as "personality ethic"

   D. can guarantee personal happiness and fulfillment

12. The inner sense of what is right and what is wrong is constituted by _____.

   A. political and legal philosophy

   B. principles and values that give the life direction, meaning and depth

   C. laws or rules of good conduct acknowledged by the society

   D. decisions based on religious doctrine

Passage 3

Ethics is the science of morals in human contact. It is that branch of philosophy concerned with the study of the conduct and character of people. It is the systematic study of the principles and methods for distinguishing right from wrong and good from bad. The word "ethics" is translation of the Greek word "ethikos". Morals and ethics are not the same thing. The word ethics refers to a set of moral principles. Morals are defined as "custom" or "folkways" that are considered conducive to the welfare of society and so, through general observance, develop into the force of law, often becoming part of the formal legal code — a set of moral principles. Morals are made by humans in their quest to control their environment. Morals are codes for survival of the individual, the family, the group and society. Morals are common sense guidelines for happier living, while ethics can be defined as the study of a moral code and the decisions one makes in one's relationships to others. Morals should be defined as a code of good conduct laid down on the basis of experience to serve as a uniform yardstick for the conduct of individuals and groups. Ethics is a personal thing. Ethics cannot be enforced. Morals can be enforced, as they tend to become the law of society. Morals are actually laws. Ethical conduct includes adherence to the moral codes of society in which we live.

Ethics has various interconnections with other branches of philosophy, such as metaphysics (the theoretical philosophy of being and knowing — the philosophy of mind), realism (the study of reality) and epistemology (the study of knowledge). This may be seen in such questions as whether there is any real difference between right and wrong and, if there is, whether it can be known.

Ethical inquiry over the centuries has revealed uncertainty about and conflict of opinions on what ought to be done and what ought not to be done. It has sometimes demonstrated the painful consequences of an action that earlier seemed perfectly acceptable but no longer complies with modern norms. It creates an awareness of differences in norms and practices among different societies. All these experiences give rise to practical questions: What should I do? Is this policy or action fair? It also gives rise to theoretical questions such as: Are any of these standards and norms (values) really right or are they arbitrary? What does it mean to say that something is right or good? What makes right actions right and wrong actions wrong? How can disputes about moral questions be resolved? It is the task of ethics to answer all such questions.

Choose the best answer according to the passage.
13. Which of the followings is NOT true about "morals"?
    A. Morals are actually different from ethics.
    B. Morals can probably develop into the force of law.
    C. Morals are formed when humans pursue the control of their environment.
    D. Morals are common sense for the survival of individuals and the society.
14. Both Ethics and Morals can be enforced. _____ (Y/N/NG)
15. Ethics is interconnected with _____ and _____.

Further Reading

The Commencement Address

Steve Jobs

Stanford, June 12, 2005

I am honored to be with you today at your commencement from one of the finest universities in the world. Truth be told, I never graduated from college. This is the closest I've ever gotten to a college graduation. Today I want to tell you three stories from my life. That's it. No big deal. Just three stories.

The first story is about connecting the dots.

I dropped out of Reed College after the first 6 months, but then stayed around as a drop-in for another 18 months or so before I really quit. So why did I drop out?

It started before I was born. My biological mother was a young, unwed college graduate student, and she decided to put me up for adoption.  She felt very strongly that I should be adopted by college graduates, so everything was all set for me to be adopted at birth by a lawyer and his wife. Except that when I popped out they decided at the last minute that they really wanted a girl. So my parents, who were on a waiting list, got a call in the middle of the night asking: "We got an unexpected baby boy; do you want him?" They said: "Of course." My biological mother found out later that my mother had never graduated from college and that my father had never graduated from high school. She refused to sign the final adoption papers. She only relented a few months later when my parents promised that I would go to college. This was the start in my life.

And 17 years later I did go to college. But I naively chose a college that was almost as expensive as Stanford, and all of my working-class parents' savings were being spent on my college tuition. After six months, I couldn't see the value in it. I had no idea what I wanted to do with my life and no idea how college was going to help me figure it out. And here I was spending all of the money my parents had saved their entire life. So I decided to drop out and trust that it would all work out OK. It was pretty scary at the time, but looking back it was one of the best decisions I ever made. The minute I dropped out I could stop taking the required classes that didn't interest me, and begin dropping in on the ones that looked far more interesting.

It wasn't all romantic. I didn't have a dorm room, so I slept on the floor in friends' rooms, I returned coke bottles for the 5 cents deposits to buy food with, and I would walk the 7 miles across town every Sunday night to get one good meal a week at the Hare Krishna temple. I loved it. And much of what I stumbled into by following my curiosity and intuition turned out to be priceless later on. Let me give you one example:

Reed College at that time offered perhaps the best calligraphy instruction in the country. Throughout the campus every poster, every label on every drawer, was beautifully hand calligraphied. Because I had dropped out and didn't have to take the normal classes, I decided to take a calligraphy class to learn how to do this. I learned about serif and san serif typefaces, about varying the amount of space between different letter combinations, about what makes great typography great. It was beautiful, historical, artistically subtle in a way that science can't capture, and I found it fascinating.

None of this had even a hope of any practical application in my life. But ten years later, when we were designing the first Macintosh computer, it all came back to me. And we designed it all into the Mac. It was the first computer with beautiful typography. If I had never dropped in on that single course in college, the Mac would have never had multiple typefaces or proportionally spaced fonts. And since Windows just copied the Mac, it's likely that no personal computer would have them. If I had never dropped out, I would have never dropped in on this calligraphy class, and personal computers might not have the wonderful typography that they do. Of course it was impossible to connect the dots looking forward when I was in college. But it was very, very clear looking backwards ten years later.

Again, you can't connect the dots looking forward; you can only connect them looking backwards. So you have to trust that the dots will somehow connect in your future. You have to trust in something — your gut, destiny, life, karma, whatever — because believing that the dots will connect down the road will give you the confidence to follow your heart, even when it leads you off the well-warmed path, and that will make all the difference.

My second story is about love and loss.

I was lucky — I found what I loved to do early in life. Woz and I started Apple in my parents garage when I was 20. We worked hard, and in 10 years Apple had grown from just the two of us in a garage into a MYM2 billion company with over 4000 employees. We had just released our finest creation — the Macintosh — a year earlier, and I had just turned 30. And then I got fired. How can you get fired from a company you started? Well, as Apple grew we hired someone who I thought was very talented to run the company with me, and for the first year or so things went well. But then our visions of the future began to diverge and eventually we had a falling out. When we did, our Board of Directors sided with him. So at 30 I was out. And very publicly out. What had been the focus of my entire adult life was gone, and it was devastating.

I really didn't know what to do for a few months. I felt that I had let the previous generation of entrepreneurs down — that I had dropped the baton as it was being passed to me. I met with David Packard and Bob Noyce and tried to apologize for screwing up so badly. I was a very public failure, and I even thought about running away from the valley. But something slowly began to dawn on me — I still loved what I did. The turn of events at Apple had not changed that one bit. I had been rejected, but I was still in love. And so I decided to start over.

I didn't see it then, but it turned out that getting fired from Apple was the best thing that could have ever happened to me. The heaviness of being successful was replaced by the lightness of being a beginner again, less sure about everything. It freed me to enter one of the most creative periods of my life.

During the next five years, I started a company named NeXT, another company named Pixar, and fell in love with an amazing woman who would become my wife. Pixar went on to create the world's first computer animated feature film, *Toy Story*, and is now the most successful animation studio in the world. In a remarkable turn of events, Apple bought NeXT, I returned to Apple, and the technology we developed at NeXT is at the heart of Apple's current renaissance. And Laurene and I have a wonderful family together.

I'm pretty sure none of this would have happened if I hadn't been fired from Apple. It was awful tasted medicine, but I guess the patient needed it. Sometimes life hits you in the head with a brick. Don't lose faith. I'm convinced that the only thing that kept me going was that I loved what I did. You've got to find what you love. And that is as true for your work as it is for your lovers. Your work is going to fill a large part of your life, and the only way to be truly satisfied is to do what you believe is great work. And the only way to do great work is to love what you do. If you haven't found it yet, keep looking and don't settle. As with all matters of the heart, you'll know when you find it. And, like any great relationship, it just gets better and better as the years roll on. So keep looking, don't settle.

My third story is about death.

When I was 17, I read a quote that went something like: "If you live each day as if it was your last, someday you'll most certainly be right." It made an impression on me, and since then, for the past 33 years, I have looked in the mirror every morning and asked myself: "If today were the last day of my life, would I want to do what I am about to do today?" And whenever the answer has been "No" for too many days in a row, I know I need to change something.

Remembering that I'll be dead soon is the most important tool I've ever encountered to help me make the big choices in life. Because almost everything — all external expectations, all pride, all fear of embarrassment or failure — these things just fall away in the face of death, leaving only what is truly important. Remembering that you are going to die is the best way I know to avoid the trap of thinking you have something to lose. You are already naked. There is no reason not to follow your heart.

About a year ago I was diagnosed with cancer. I had a scan at 7:30 in the morning, and it clearly showed a tumor on my pancreas. I didn't even know what a pancreas was. The doctors told me this was almost certainly a type of cancer that is incurable, and that I should expect to live no longer than three to six months. My doctor advised me to go home and get my affairs in order, which is doctor's code for prepare to die. It means to try to tell your kids everything you thought you'd have the next 10 years to tell them in just a few months. It means to make sure everything is buttoned up so that it will be as easy as possible for your family. It means to say your goodbyes.

I lived with that diagnosis all day. Later that evening I had a biopsy, where they stuck an endoscope down my throat, through my stomach and into my intestines, put a needle into my pancreas and got a few cells from the tumor. I was sedated, but my wife, who was there, told me that when they viewed the cells under a microscope the doctors started crying because it turned out to be a very rare form of pancreatic cancer that is curable with surgery. I had the surgery and thankfully, I'm fine now.

This was the closest I've been to facing death, and I hope it's the closest I get for a few more decades. Having lived through it, I can now say this to you with a bit more certainty than when death was a useful but purely intellectual concept:

No one wants to die. Even people who want to go to heaven don't want to die to get there. And yet death is the destination we all share. No one has ever escaped it. And that is as it should be, because Death is very likely the single best invention of Life. It is Life's change agent. It clears out the old to make way for the new. Right now the new is you, but someday not too long from now, you will gradually become the old and be cleared away. Sorry to be so dramatic, but it is quite true.

Your time is limited, so don't waste it living someone else's life. Don't be trapped by dogma — which is living with the results of other people's thinking. Don't let the noise of other's opinions drown out your own inner voice. And most important, have the courage to follow your heart and intuition. They somehow already know what you truly want to become. Everything else is secondary.

When I was young, there was an amazing publication called *The Whole Earth Catalog*, which was one of the bibles of my generation. It was created by a fellow named Stewart Brand not far from here in Menlo Park, and he brought it to life with his poetic touch. This was in the late 1960's, before personal computers and desktop publishing, so it was all made with typewriters, scissors, and polaroid cameras. It was sort of like Google in paperback form, 35 years before Google came along: it was idealistic, and overflowing with neat tools and great notions.

Stewart and his team put out several issues of *The Whole Earth Catalog*, and then when it had run its course, they put out a final issue. It was the mid-1970s, and I was your age. On the back cover of their final issue was a photograph of an early morning country road, the kind you might find yourself hitchhiking on if you were so adventurous. Beneath it were the words: "Stay Hungry. Stay Foolish." It was their farewell message as they signed off. Stay Hungry. Stay Foolish. And I have always wished that for myself. And now, as you graduate to begin anew, I wish that for you.

Stay Hungry. Stay Foolish.

Thank you all very much.

I. Read the passage above and decide whether the statement is true (T) or false (F).

1. _____ Steve Jobs quitted school because he thought the courses at Reed College were too hard to follow.
2. _____ Steve Jobs' biological mother refused to sign the adoption papers because she thought the couple were not able to give him good education.
3. _____ Steve Jobs was fired from Apple because he didn't run the business well.
4. _____ Steve Jobs attributed his success to his decision to quit school at an early age.
5. _____ Steve Jobs thought that the dots one collected were meaningful only if they were looked backwards.
6. _____ The turn of events at Apple at his 30 changed Steve's curiosity and research interests.
7. _____ If you live each day as if it was your last, you can make your decisions more rapidly and firmly.
8. _____ Steve Jobs followed the doctor's advice to prepare for the death immediately when he was diagnosed with cancer.

II. Discussion & mini-presentation.

1. Do you agree with Steve Jobs that "Death is very likely the single best invention of Life"? Discuss first in your team and then present your arguments to the class.

   _____
   _____

2. Discuss with your classmates about the reasons for Steve Jobs' success. Give a mini-presentation on "Stay Hungry. Stay Foolish".

   _____
   _____
   _____

Unit 8

Man's Peril

Bertrand Russell

I am speaking on this occasion not as a Briton, not as a European, not as a member of a Western democracy, but as a human being, a member of the species Man, whose continued existence is in doubt. The world is full of conflicts: Jews and Arabs; Indians and Pakistanis; white men and negroes in Africa; and, overshadowing all minor conflicts, the titanic struggle between Communism and anti-Communism.

Almost everybody who is politically conscious has strong feelings about one or more of these issues; but I want you, if you can, to set aside such feelings for the moment and consider yourself only as a member of a biological species which has had a remarkable history and whose disappearance none of us can desire. I shall try to say no single word which should appeal to one group rather than to another. All, equally, are in peril and, if the peril is understood, there is hope that they may collectively avert it. We have to learn to think in a new way. We have to learn to ask ourselves not what steps can be taken to give military victory to whatever group we prefer, for there no-longer are such steps. The question we have to ask ourselves is: What steps can be taken to prevent a military contest of which the issue must be disastrous to all sides?

The general public, and even many men in positions of authority, have not realized what would be involved in a war with hydrogen bombs. The general public still thinks in terms of the obliteration of cities. It is understood that the new bombs are more powerful than the old and that, while one atomic bomb could obliterate Hiroshima, one hydrogen bomb could obliterate the largest cities such as London, New York, and Moscow. No doubt in a hydrogen-bomb war great cities would be obliterated. But this is one of the minor disasters that would have to be faced. If everybody in London, New York, and

Moscow were exterminated, the world might, in the course of a few centuries, recover from the blow.

But we now know, especially since the Bikini test, that hydrogen bombs can gradually spread destruction over a much wider area than had been supposed. It is stated on very good authority that a bomb can now be manufactured which will be 25,000 times as powerful as that which destroyed Hiroshima. Such a bomb, if exploded near the ground or under water, sends radio-active particles into the upper air. They sink gradually and reach the surface of the earth in the form of a deadly dust or rain. It was this dust which infected the Japanese fishermen and their catch of fish although they were outside what American experts believed to be the danger zone. No one knows how widely such lethal radio-active particles might be diffused, but the best authorities are unanimous in saying that a war with hydrogen bombs is quite likely to put an end to the human race. It is feared that if many hydrogen bombs are used there will be universal death — sudden only for a fortunate minority, but for the majority a slow torture of disease and disintegration.

I will give a few instances out of many. Sir John Slessor, who can speak with unrivalled authority from his experiences of air warfare, has said: "A world war in this day and age would be general suicide"; and has gone on to state: "It never has and never will make any sense trying to abolish any particular weapon of war. What we have got to abolish is war." Lord Adrian, who is the leading English authority on nerve physiology, recently emphasized the same point in his address as President of the British Association. He said: "We must face the possibility that repeated atomic explosions will lead to a degree of general radio-activity which no one can tolerate or escape"; and he added: "Unless we are ready to give up some of our old loyalties, we may be forced into a fight which might end the human race." Air Chief Marshal Sir Philip Joubert says: "With the advent of the hydrogen bomb, it would appear that the human race has arrived at a point where it must abandon war as a continuation of policy or accept the possibility of total destruction." I could prolong such quotations indefinitely.

Many warnings have been uttered by eminent men of science and by authorities in military strategy. None of them will say that the worst results are certain. What they do say is that these results are possible and no one can be sure that they will not be realized. I have not found that the views of experts on this question depend in any degree upon their politics or prejudices. They depend only, so far as my researches have revealed, upon the extent of the particular expert's knowledge. I have found that the men who know most are most gloomy.

Here, then, is the problem which I present to you, stark and dreadful and inescapable: Shall we put an end to the human race; or shall mankind renounce war? People will not face this alternative because it is so difficult to abolish war. The abolition of war will demand distasteful limitations of national sovereignty. But what perhaps impedes understanding of the situation more than anything else is that the term "mankind" feels vague man's peril and abstract. People scarcely realize in imagination that the danger is to themselves and their children and their grandchildren, and not only to a dimly apprehended humanity. And so they hope that perhaps war may be allowed to continue provided modern weapons are prohibited. I am afraid this hope is illusory. Whatever agreements not to use hydrogen bombs had been reached in time of peace, they would no longer be considered binding in time of war, and both sides would set to work to manufacture hydrogen bombs as soon as war broke out, for if one side manufactured the bombs and the other did not, the side that manufactured them would inevitably be victorious.

On both sides of the Iron Curtain there are political obstacles to emphasis on the destructive character of future war. If either side were to announce that it would on no account resort to war, it would be diplomatically at the mercy of the other side. Each side, for the sake of self-preservation, must continue to say that there are provocations that it will not endure. Each side may long for an  accommodation, but neither side dare express this longing convincingly. The position is analogous to that of duellists in former times. No doubt it frequently happened that each of the duellists feared death and desired an accommodation, but neither could say so, since, if he did, he would be thought a coward. The only hope in such cases was intervention by friends of both parties suggesting an accommodation to which both could agree at the same moment. This is an exact analogy to the present position of the protagonists on either side of the Iron Curtain. If an agreement making war improbable is to be reached, it will have to be by the friendly offices of neutrals, who can speak of the disastrousness of war without being accused of advocating a policy of "appeasement". The neutrals have every right, even from the narrowest consideration of self-interest, to do whatever lies in their power to prevent the outbreak of a world war, for if such a war does break out, it is highly probable that all the inhabitants of neutral countries, along with the rest of mankind, will perish. If I were in control of a neutral government, I should certainly consider it my paramount duty to see to it that my country would continue to have inhabitants, and the only way by which I could make this probable would be to promote some kind of accommodation between the powers on opposite sides of the Iron Curtain.

I, personally, am of course not neutral in my feeling and I should not wish to see the danger of war averted by an abject submission of the West. But, as a human being, I have to remember that, if the issues between East and West are to be decided in any manner that can give any possible satisfaction to anybody, whether Communist or anti-Communist, whether Asian or European or American, whether white or black, then these issues must not be decided by war. I should wish this to be understood on both sides of the Iron Curtain. It is emphatically not enough to have it understood on one side only. I think the neutrals, since they are not caught in our tragic dilemma, can, if they will, bring about this realization on both sides. I should like to see one or more neutral powers appoint a commission of experts, who should all be neutrals, to draw up a report on the destructive effects to be expected in a war with hydrogen bombs, not only among the belligerents but also among neutrals. I should wish this report presented to the Governments of all the Great Powers with an invitation to express their agreement or disagreement with its findings. I think it possible that in this way all the Great Powers could be led to agree that a world war can no longer serve the purposes of any of them, since it is likely to exterminate friend and foe equally and neutrals likewise.

As geological time is reckoned, man has so far existed only for a very short period — 1,000,000 years at the most. What he has achieved, especially during the last 6,000 years, is something utterly new in the history of the cosmos, so far at least as we are acquainted with it. For countless ages the sun rose and set, the moon waxed and waned, the stars shone in the night, but it was only with the coming of man that these things were understood. In the great world of astronomy and in the little world of the atom, man has unveiled secrets which might have been thought undiscoverable. In art and literature and religion, some men have shown a <u>sublimity</u> of feeling which makes the species worth preserving. Is all this to end in trivial horror because so few are able to think of man rather than of this or that group of men? Is our race so destitute of wisdom, so incapable of impartial love, so blind even to the simplest dictates of self-preservation, that the last proof of its silly cleverness is to be the extermination of all life on our planet? — for it will be not only men who will perish, but also the animals, whom no one can accuse of Communism or anti-Communism.

I cannot believe that this is to be the end. I would have men forget their quarrels for a moment and reflect that, if they will allow themselves to survive, there is every reason to expect the triumphs of the future to exceed immeasurably the triumpha of the past. There lies before us, if we choose, continual progress in happiness, knowledge, and wisdom. Shall we, instead, choose death, because we cannot forget our quarrels? I appeal as a human being to human beings: remember your humanity, and forget the rest. If you can do so, the way lies open to a new Paradise; if you cannot, nothing lies before you but universal death.

(Text source: This speech was given to BBC Broadcast on December 30, 1954.)

Section A: Text-based Reading Comprehension

I. Choose the best answer according to the passage.

1. Human perils can be avoided only if it is _____.
   A. identified   B. evaluated   C. understood   D. minimized
2. Why does the author believe that the hope to continue war without modern weapons is an illusion?
   A. Because modern weapons are too expensive.
   B. Because modern weapons are only controlled by very few countries.
   C. Because modern weapons could only be abandoned in the time of peace.
   D. Because modern weapons can bring the owners victory during the war.
3. What does the word "sublimity" (Para. 10) mean in the passage?
   A. Much   B. Gravity   C. Loftiness   D. Terror
4. What is the greatest peril for Man?
   A. Renouncement of war   B. Regional conflicts
   C. Atomic bomb   D. Poverty
5. What is the main purpose of this speech?
   A. To tell people to realize the danger of war
   B. To persuade Man to stop using nuclear weapon
   C. To call on Man to stop war
   D. To show the perils of human being

II. Answer the following questions.

1. What are the Man's perils discussed in the text?
   _____
   _____

2. What are the dangers of modern weapons based on the text?
   _____

III. Further discussion.

1. Benjamin Franklin once said "There was never a good war or a bad peace". How do you understand it?

2. What does the sentence "Remember your humanity, and forget the rest" mean in the final paragraph?

Section B: Vocabulary

I. Fill in the blanks with the proper forms of the words given below.

overshadow	avert	obliterate	exterminate	diffuse
unrivalled	unanimous	peril	renounce	infect
abolition	unveil	destitute	utter	stark

1. Staff use the poison to _____ moles and rabbits.
2. Edward _____ his claim to the French throne.
3. The tragedy could have been _____ if the crew had followed safety procedures.
4. As he was _____ of any other means of defense, his safety now depended entirely on bodily strength and resolution.
5. But the unlucky suggestion met with fierce and _____ opposition.
6. Media focus on the Province's death tally has tended to _____ other statistics of Northern Ireland.
7. The memorial to those who had died in the war was _____ in 1948 by the Queen.
8. Perhaps she gets drunk to _____ painful memories.
9. Television is a powerful means of _____ knowledge.
10. An Illinois House committee voted Thursday to _____ the death penalty.
11. The museum boasts a(n) _____ collection of French porcelain.
12. I never felt that my life was in _____.
13. Her optimism seemed to _____ all those around her.
14. The _____ reality is that we are operating at a huge loss.
15. She sat through the whole meeting without _____ a word.

II. Root and word formation.

A. Study the following roots and list more examples in the space provided.

Root	Meaning	Examples	More examples
-vac	empty	vacate, vacant, vacuum	
-var	change	variable, invariable	
-ven (vent)	to come	advent, intervene, event	
-ver	true	aver, verify, verily	
	to feel awe to fear	irreverent, revere	

B. Fill in the blanks with the proper forms of the words given below.

advent	vacate	prevent	evacuate
convene	revere	variable	verify

1. What can we do to _____ this disease from spreading?
2. The winds today will be light and _____.
3. The police are _____ the prisoner's statement by questioning several witnesses.
4. You must _____ the hotel room by Friday.
5. The chairman _____ a city council meeting to decide on the problem.
6. Society has changed rapidly since the _____ of the car.
7. She _____ her father all her life.
8. The village was _____ because of the danger of a flood.

Section C: Cloze

Fill in the blanks with the proper forms of the words given below.

as	teach	inherit	without	however
except	similar	water	than	in

Most primates do not shape their environment in an adaptive way. They use it __1__ it is without modification. The sleeping nests of the great apes are poor, roofless constructions created for only one night. Monkeys simply sleep on convenient tree branches __2__ making nests. No primate other __3__ humans is known to store food. They have a hand-to-mouth economy which forces everyone to seek food and water daily. However, adult male chimpanzees and adult bonobos of both genders cooperate with others in their community __4__ hunting monkeys and other small game. While they do not store the meat, they do use it for social gain by sharing it. Jane Goodall has observed a chimpanzee carry a carcass as far as a mile over grasslands to reach the safety of trees before eating it.

Tool manufacture and use are virtually non-existent among non-human primates. __5__, gorillas, common chimpanzees, bonobos, orangutans, and capuchin monkeys are notable __6__. Some of them use very simple tools to help in acquiring food and water. For instance, chimpanzees have been observed stripping the leaves from twigs to make probes to get termites and ants to eat. They use __7__ modified sticks to obtain honey from beehives in tree trunks and from up to a meter underground in subterranean hives. Twigs are also used by them at times as toothpicks. Crinkled leaves are employed as sponges to get __8__ from hollows in trees for drinking. Rocks and broken tree branches are used to crack nuts and sometimes to throw at other chimpanzees in order to intimidate them. Rocks are used at times as projectiles in hunting bush pigs and other small game. However, chimpanzee coordination in throwing is very poor, so rocks and pieces of wood are inefficient weapons for them. Their easy excitability also prevents them from being stealthy hunters. It is important to keep in mind that all of these very simple tool uses by chimpanzees must be __9__ to children by their parents and other adults. They are not genetically __10__ patterns of behavior. As a result, different communities invent different tools. It would not be surprising to discover other examples of simple tool use by non-human primates as more species are carefully observed for long periods of time.

Section D: Reading Skills Training

Directions: The following exercises are meant to improve your fast reading ability. And you are suggested to go over the passages quickly and then answer all the questions within 25 minutes.

Passage 1
For questions 1 - 7, please mark
 Y (for YES) if the statement agrees with the information given in the passage;
 N (for NO) if the statement contradicts the information given in the passage;
 NG (for NOT GIVEN) if the statement is not given in the passage.
For questions 8 - 10, complete the sentences with the information given in the passage.
1. _____ Mills can manage to graduate on time although he has to deal with so many tasks at the same time.
2. _____ It is getting harder for students to get face-to-face advising as a number of advisers have retired and caseloads soar.
3. _____ Complete College America reports that on average students get 16.5 credits more than the credit requirement of bachelor's degree.

4. _____ According to Anthony Carnevale, too many students are confused about what to do and it is very important for them to know where they're going.
5. _____ Davis Jenkins says that some community-college students graduate by design instead of graduating by accident.
6. _____ If a student fails to finish a required course or may fall below a certain grade-point average, eAdvisor will tell him so in big red letters and sends him off to see a face-to-face adviser.
7. _____ Arizona State's eAdvisor is now being applied in all the U. S. universities and colleges.
8. The eAdvisor frees real-life advisers at Arizona State from the drudgery of _____.
9. The eAdvisor tracks whether students can do well in subjects that are _____.
10. According to Phillips, the university is making efforts to make eAdvisor more _____.

Student advising plays a key role in college success

TEMPE, Arizona — Devon Mills pulls out his smartphone at a Starbucks on the Arizona State University campus and maps out how long it will take him to finish his undergraduate degree.

Just exactly the right amount of time, his phone tells him.

In spite of double-majoring in political science and justice studies with a minor in sustainability, serving as president of the college council and vice president of the Residence Hall Association, working as a page in the state Senate, and cramming for the Law School Admission Test, Mills is on schedule to become one of the distinct minority of American university and college students who actually receive their four-year bachelor's degrees in four years.

"I can see the goal in sight," he says, serenely scrolling through an online color-coded plan that shows him the requirements he's finished and the ones he still needs to fulfill before graduating in 2014.

While academics are debating whether students can effectively learn online, the program Mills is using harnesses technology to provide something else that is surprisingly essential to success in college: advising that can help prevent an education from slipping off track.

"The research clearly shows that when a student is more engaged on a campus they are more likely to remain enrolled and persist to graduation," says Charlie Nutt, executive director of the National Academic Advising Association, or NACADA. "Academic advising is the key mechanism, and on many campuses the only mechanism, through which students have a person they're connected with."

But just when it seems to be needed most, face-to-face advising is getting harder for students to find as the number of advisers shrinks and caseloads soar because of budget cuts and enrollment increases.

U. S. universities had, on average, one adviser for every 367 students last year, down from one for every 282 in 2003, according to a survey by NACADA and the college-admissions testing company ACT. Though more students than ever work to pay tuition and expenses, advisers are seldom available at night or on weekends. And waits for appointments during business hours can stretch for weeks.

Piling up unneeded credits

As a result, many students flounder through college, changing majors, piling up and paying for credits they don't need, and taking more time than they planned to graduate.

On average, students rack up 136.5 credits toward bachelor's degrees that require only 120, the advocacy organization Complete College America reports. One of every three switches majors, according to the Higher Education Research Institute at UCLA. And the Department of Education's National Center for Education Statistics says that fewer than one in four students at public universities, and around a third at private ones, graduate within four years.

"There's too much wandering around," says Anthony Carnevale, director of the Georgetown University Center on Education and the Workforce. "It makes sense that if you know where you're going, you're more likely to get there."

The picture is even worse at community colleges, whose students are particularly likely to struggle. Academic counselors at community colleges typically handle 1,000 students each, according to MDRC, a nonprofit research organization. In some cash-strapped California community colleges, the ratio is as high as one to 1,700.

Half of community-college students don't even know advising is available to them, says Davis Jenkins, a researcher at the Community College Research Center at Columbia University's Teachers College. The one-third of them who finish their two-year programs within even three years take, on average, 80 credits toward associate degrees they could have gotten with just 60, according to Complete College America.

"We have a situation of almost completion by accident rather than completion by design," says Jenkins.

The problem has grown more urgent as the type of student changes. More students today are older than traditional age, or the first in their families to go to college, or they attend part time while working or raising children of their own.

That makes navigating the bureaucracy of higher education even harder than it already was. Arizona State, for instance, offers 250 majors, and 3,071 undergraduate courses — many with prerequisites that, in turn, have their own prerequisites.

Even 18-year-olds who come from college-going families are so overscheduled by helicopter parents in their earlier grades that they struggle when they're set free in college.

"They have to learn to manage time," says Nutt, who is also a professor of education at Kansas State University. "An adviser is essential to that."

Turning to technology

In focus groups, students say they just want someone to tell them what to do, says Shanna Jaggars, also of the Community College Research Center.

Or if not someone, at least something.

Arizona State's eAdvisor, which was launched in 2008, puts the information students need online, night and day, and follows their progress as a live adviser would.

"We've waited too long to use technology in this way," says the university's president, Michael Crow.

Students start by entering their interests, search engine-style — "I like to work with people," for example, or, "I would like to do something with music" — and eAdvisor helps them pick a major. Each then gets a "major map," which charts a trail through the complicated combination of requirements. If a student wanders off the trail by failing to finish a required course or threatening to fall below a certain grade-point average, eAdvisor tells him so, in big red letters, and sends him off to see a face-to-face adviser.

The results have been dramatic. The proportion of freshmen who don't return for sophomore year has fallen from 24 percent to 16 percent, much lower than the national average, and 42 percent graduate in four years — up from less than 26 percent in 1997, and almost double the proportion at public universities nationwide.

"It's about looking at universities from the perspective of the students," says Elizabeth Phillips, the provost, who first introduced a form of eAdvisor when she worked at the University of Florida and brought it with her to Arizona State.

Human advisers are expensive, error prone and soft, says Phillips, whose academic field is psychology. Part of advising, she says, is taking the hard line of "telling a kid they're not going to be what they thought they were going to be." There are still real-life advisers at Arizona State. But eAdvisor frees them from the drudgery of scheduling courses. "By the time you go in to see your face-to-face adviser, you can focus on strategy and life issues," Crow says.

The eAdvisor system helps in other ways, too. Since students are planning their courses in advance, it helps the university provide the right number of seats. Not being able to get into required courses is another reason students take so long to graduate at other universities. At Arizona State, administrators say and students confirm, it almost never happens.

The system tracks whether students do well in the kinds of subjects that are essential to careers they want. If they want to major in psychology, for instance, it makes them take statistics first — and if they don't do well, suggests that they consider other majors. If they're in danger of failing, it freezes their ability to continue until they meet with an in-person counselor.

There are other ways the university is using technology to track its students — and, for that matter, its advisors. Phillips gets a report if an adviser gives too many overrides, for example, waiving prerequisites or restrictions on class sizes. The system also captures information from the financial-aid and residence-hall offices, the campus police department, and judicial boards about financial or behavior problems students might be running into.

"Now we're a machine, to provide the kids exactly what they need," says Phillips.

There are some shortcomings. Meant to be simple to use, eAdvisor seems at first glance almost indecipherable.

"When I first looked through it, I was a little confused," says Steven Denke, a senior electrical-engineering major in the honors college who had to take five different technical electives, plus the university's core requirements, and transfer credits from advanced-placement and dual-enrollment courses that he passed in high school. "It was daunting at first, just looking at the major map."

Phillips says the university is working on making eAdvisor more user friendly. Adds Crow: "What we have is a very early precursor of where this is going to go."

Christina Arregoces, a junior majoring in English and creative writing, likes being able to monitor her progress at any time.

"I'm one of those people who double-checks everything," Arregoces says. "It's nice to have a map so you know what you're doing and what you need to do."

Passage 2

Critics continually debate literature's chief function. Tracing their arguments to Plato, many contend that literature's primary function is moral, its chief value being its usefulness for cultural or societal purposes. But others, like Aristotle, hold that a work of art can be analyzed and broken down into its various parts, with each part contributing to the overall enjoyment of the work itself. For these critics, the value of a text is found within the text itself or is inseparably linked to the work itself. In its most simple terms, the debate centers around two concerns: Is literature's chief function to teach (extrinsic) or to entertain (intrinsic)? In other words, can we read a text for the sheer fun of it, or must we always be studying and learning from what we read?

Such questions and their various answers lead us directly to literary theory, for literary theory concerns itself not only with ontological questions (whether a text really exists), but also with epistemological issues (how we know or ways of knowing). When we ask, then, if literature's chief function is to entertain or to teach, we are really asking epistemological questions. Whether we read a text to learn from it or to be entertained, we can say that once we have read a text we "know" that text.

We can know a text, however, in two distinct ways. The first way involves the typical literature classroom analysis. When we have studied, analyzed, and critiqued a text and arrived at an interpretation, we can then confidently assert that we know the text. On the other hand, when we stay up all night turning the pages of P. D. James's mystery novel *Death in Holy Orders* to discover who the murderer is, we can also say that we know the text, for we have spent time devouring its pages, lost in its secondary world, consumed by its characters. Both methods — one with its chief goal to learn, the other to entertain — involve similar yet distinct epistemological endpoints: to know a text, but in two different ways.

Choose the best answer according to the passage.
11. Which one of the followings is not mentioned as the chief function of literature?
    A. Moral functions   B. To debate   C. To entertain   D. To teach
12. When the author mentions P. D. James's novel *Death in Holy Order*, he intends to say that _____.
    A. the novel is fit for literature classroom analysis
    B. the novel is an interesting one
    C. readers will be attracted by this kind of novel
    D. the novel is an example of literature's chief function to entertain

Passage 3

The French verb *savoir* and *connaître* can both be translated "to know" and can highlight for us the difference between these two epistemological goals or ways of knowing a text. *Savoir* means "to analyze" (from the Greek analuetin, to undo) and "to study". The word is used to refer to knowing something that is the object study and assumes that the object, such as a text, can be examined, analyzed, and critiqued. Knowledge or learning about is the ultimate goal.

Connaître, on the other hand, implied that we intimately know or have experienced the text. Interestingly, *connaître* is used for knowing people and refers also to knowing an author's canon. Both knowing persons and knowing all a writer's works imply intimacy, learning the particular qualities of one person or author, ins and outs of each. Indeed, it is this intimacy that one often experiences while reading a mystery novel all night along. It is knowing or knowledge of that the word means.

To know how to analyze a text, to discuss its literary elements, and to apply the various methodologies of literary criticism means that we know that text (*savoir*). To have experienced the text, to have cried with or about its characters, to have lost time and sleep immersed in the secondary world of the text, and to have felt our emotions stirred also means that we know that text (*connaître*). From one way of knowing, we learn facts or information; from the other, we encounter and participate in an intimate experience.

At times, however, we have actually known the text from both these perspectives, *savoir* and *connaître*. While analyzing and critiquing a text (*savoir*), we have at times (perhaps more often then not) simultaneously experienced it, becoming emotionally involved with its characters' choices and destinies (*connaître*) and imagining ourselves to be these characters — or at least recognizing some of our own characteristics dramatized by the characters.

To say that we know a text is no simple statement. Underlying our private and public reactions and our scholarly critiques and analyses is our literary theory, the fountainhead of our most intimate and our most public declarations. The formal study of literary theory therefore enables us to explain our responses to any text and allows us to articulate the function of literature in an academic and a personal way. Then why is a study of literary study essential?

- Literary theory assumes that there is no such thing as an innocent reading of a text. Whether our responses are emotional and spontaneous or well reasoned and highly structured, all such interactions with and about a text are based on some underlying factors that cause us to respond to that text in a particular fashion. What elicits these responses or how a reader makes sense of a text is at the heart of literary theory.
- Because our reactions to any text have theoretical bases, all readers must have a literary theory. The methods we use to frame our personal interpretations of any text directly involve us in the process of literary criticism and theory, automatically making us practicing literary critics.
- Many readers have a literary theory that is more often than not unconscious, incomplete, ill informed, and eclectic; therefore their interpretations can easily be illogical, unsound, and haphazard. A well-defined, logical, and clearly articulated literary theory enables readers to consciously develop their own methods of interpretation, permitting them to order, clarify, and justify their appraisals of a text in a consistent and logical manner.

Choose the best answer according to the passage.
13. What does the underlined word "intimacy" in Paragraph 2 probably mean?
    A. Close familiarity   B. Mutual interaction
    C. Intellectual skill   D. Literary piracy
14. Which of the following sayings about *connaître* is true?
    A. *Connaître* can be also translated "to know", "to analyze" and "to study".
    B. *Connaître* assumes that a text can be examined, analyzed and critiqued.
    C. *Connaître*'s ultimate goal is knowledge.
    D. *Connaître* implies that we intimately know that text.

15. The reasons why we should study a literary theory include the following except ____.
    A. Literary theory assumes that innocent reading of a text does exist among readers.
    B. How a reader makes sense of a text is at the heart of literary theory.
    C. Because our reactions to any text have theoretical bases, all readers must have a literary theory.
    D. A well-defined, logical and clearly articulated literary theory is probably necessary for readers.

Further Reading

The Road to Success (Excerpt)

Andrew Carnegie

It is well that young men should begin at the beginning and occupy the most subordinate positions. Many of the leading business men of Pittsburg had a serious responsibility thrust upon them at the very threshold of their career. They were introduced to the broom, and spent the first hours of their business lives sweeping out the office. I notice we have janitors and janitresses now in offices, and our young men unfortunately miss that salutary branch of a business education. But if by chance the professional sweeper is absent any morning the boy who has the genius of the future partner in him will not hesitate to try his hand at the broom. The other day a fond fashionable mother in Michigan asked a young man whether he had ever seen a young lady sweep in a room so grandly as her Priscilla. He said no, he never had, and the mother was gratified beyond measure, but then said he, after a pause, "What I should like to see her do is sweep out a room." It does not hurt the newest comer to sweep out the office if necessary. I was one of those sweepers myself.

Assuming that you have all obtained employment and are fairly started, my advice to you is "aim high." I would not give a fig for the young man who does not already see himself the partner or the head of an important firm. Do not rest content for a moment in your thoughts as head clerk, or foreman, or general manager in any concern, no matter how extensive. Say each to yourself. "My place is at the top." *Be king in your dreams.* Make your vow that you will reach that position, with untarnished reputation, and make no other vow to distract your attention, except the very commendable one that when you are a member of the firm or before that, if you have been promoted two or three times, you will form another partnership with the loveliest of her sex — a partnership to which our new partnership act has no application. The liability there is never limited.

Let me indicate two or three conditions essential to success. Do not be afraid that I am going to moralize, or inflict a homily upon you. I speak upon the subject only from the view of a man of the world, desirous of aiding you to become successful business men. You all know that there is no genuine, praiseworthy success in life if you are not honest, truthful, fair-dealing. I assume you are and will remain all these, and also that you are determined to live pure, respectable lives, free from pernicious or equivocal associations with one sex or the other. There is no creditable future for you else. Otherwise your learning and your advantages not only go for naught, but serve to accentuate your failure and your disgrace. I hope you will not take it amiss if I warn you against three of the gravest dangers which will beset you in your upward path.

The first and most seductive, and the destroyer of most young men, is the drinking of liquor. I am no temperance lecturer in disguise, but a man who knows and tells you what observation has proved to him, and I say to you that you are more likely to fail in your career from acquiring the habit of drinking liquor than from any, or all, the other temptations likely to assail you. You may yield to almost any other temptation and reform — may brace up, and if not recover lost ground, at least remain in the race and secure and maintain a respectable position. But from the insane thirst for liquor escape is almost impossible. I have known but few exceptions to this rule. First, then, you must not drink liquor to excess. Better if you do not touch it at all — much better; but if this be too hard a rule for you then take your stand firmly here. Resolve never to touch it except at meals. A glass at dinner will not hinder your advance in life or lower your tone; but I implore you hold it inconsistent with the dignity and self-respect of gentlemen, with what is due from yourselves to yourselves, being the men you are, and especially the men you are determined to become, to drink a glass of liquor at a bar. Be far too much of the gentleman ever to enter a barroom. You do not pursue your careers in safety unless you stand firmly upon this ground. Adhere to it and you have escaped danger from the deadliest of your foes.

The next greatest danger to a young business man in this community I believe to be that of speculation. When I was a telegraph operator here we had no Exchanges in the City, but the men or firms who speculated upon the Eastern Exchanges were necessarily known to the operators. They could be counted on the fingers of one hand. These men were not our citizens of first repute; they were regarded with suspicion. I have lived to see all of these speculators irreparably ruined men, bankrupt in money and bankrupt in character. There is scarcely an instance of a man who has made a fortune by speculation and kept it. Gamesters die poor, and there is certainly not an instance of a speculator who has lived a life creditable to himself, or advantageous to the community. The man who grasps the morning paper to see first how his speculative ventures upon the Exchanges are likely to result, unfits himself for the calm consideration and proper solution of business problems, with which he has to deal later in the day, and saps the sources of that persistent and concentrated energy upon which depend the permanent success, and often the very safety, of his main business.

The speculator and the business man tread diverging lines. The former depends upon the sudden turn of fortune's wheel; he is a millionaire today, a bankrupt tomorrow. But the man of business knows that only by years of patient, unremitting attention to affairs can he earn his reward, which is the result, not of chance, but of well-devised means for the attainment of ends. During all these years his is the cheering thought that, by no possibility can he benefit himself without carrying prosperity to others. The speculator on the other hand had better never have lived so far as the good of others or the good of the community is concerned. Hundreds of young men were tempted in this city not long since to gamble in oil, and many were ruined; all were injured whether they lost or won. You may be, nay, you are certain to be similarly tempted; but when so tempted I hope you will remember this advice. Say to the tempter who asks you to risk your small savings, that if ever you decide to speculate you are determined to go to a regular and well-conducted house where they cheat fair. You can get fair play and about an equal chance upon the red and black in such a place; upon the Exchange you have neither. You might as well try your luck with the three-card-monte man. There is another point involved in speculation. Nothing is more essential to young business men than untarnished credit, credit begotten of confidence in their prudence, principles and stability of character. Well, believe me, nothing kills credit sooner in any Bank Board than the knowledge that either firms or men engage in speculation. It matters not a whit whether gains or losses be the temporary result of these operations. The moment a man is known to speculate, his credit is impaired, and soon thereafter it is gone. How can a man be credited whose resources may be swept away in one hour by a panic among gamesters? Who can tell how he stands among them? Except that this is certain: he has given due notice that he may stand to lose all, so that those who credit him have themselves to blame. Resolve to be business men, but speculators never.

The third and last danger against which I shall warn you is one which has wrecked many a fair craft which started well and gave promise of a prosperous voyage. It is the perilous habit of indorsing — all the more dangerous, inasmuch as it assails one generally in the garb of friendship. It appeals to your generous instincts, and you say, "How can I refuse to lend my name only, to assist a friend?" It is because there is so much that is true and commendable in that view that the practice is so dangerous. Let me endeavor to put you upon safe honourable grounds in regard to it. I would say to you to make it a rule now, never indorse: but this is too much like never taste wine, or never smoke, or any other of the "nevers." They generally result in exceptions. You will as business men now and then probably become security for friends. Now, here is the line at which regard for the success of friends should cease and regard for your own honour begins.

If you owe anything, all your capital and all your effects are a solemn trust in your hands to be held inviolate for the security of those who have trusted you. Nothing can be done by you with honour which jeopardizes these first claims upon you. When a man in debt indorses for another, it is not his own credit or his own capital he risks, it is that of his own creditors. He violates a trust. Mark you then, never indorse until you have cash means not required for your own debts, and never indorse beyond those means. Before you indorse at all, consider indorsements as gifts, and ask yourselves whether you wish to make the gift to your friend and whether the money is really yours to give and not a trust for your creditors.

You are not safe, gentlemen, unless you stand firmly upon this as the only ground which an honest business man can occupy.

I beseech you avoid liquor, speculation and indorsement. Do not fail in either, for liquor and speculation are the Scylla and Charybdis of the young man's business sea, and indorsement his rock ahead.

I. Read the passage above and decide whether the statement is true (T) or false (F).

1. _____ Young graduates should start their career with trivial jobs such as sweepers.
2. _____ According to the author, young men had better not drink liquor, because it is the first and most destructive for them.
3. _____ There are a lot of people who have made a fortune by speculation.
4. _____ For most successful businessmen, business is a matter of chance and the sudden turn of fortune's wheel.
5. _____ You can indorse when you have cash means not required for your own debts, and never indorse beyond those means.
6. _____ The three dangers stated in the text are equally destructive for one's success. One cannot fail in anyone of them.
7. _____ In the Bank Board, the knowledge in speculation outweighs others in killing your credits.

8. _____ There are exceptions for indorsement in business.

II. Discussion & mini-presentation.

1. Do you agree with the author that liquor, speculation and indorsement are the three main factors that prevent one from business success? In your opinion, what is the key to business success?

   _____

   _____

2. Andrew Carnegie holds the belief that the rich should use their wealth to help enrich society. He once said "The man who dies thus rich dies disgraced". Should rich people donate all their wealth to the society before they die? Discuss it with your team members and then present your view to the class.

   _____

   _____

Unit 9

Third Inaugural Address

Franklin D. Roosevelt.

January 20, 1941.

Mr. Chief Justice, my friends:

On each national day of inauguration since 1789, the people have renewed their sense of dedication to the United States.

In Washington's day the task of the people was to create and weld together a nation.

In Lincoln's day the task of the people was to preserve that Nation from disruption from within.

In this day the task of the people is to save that Nation and its institutions from disruption from without.

To us there has come a time, in the midst of swift happenings, to pause for a moment and take stock — to recall what our place in history has been, and to rediscover what we are and what we may be. If we do not, we risk the real peril of isolation, the real peril of inaction.

Lives of nations are determined not by the count of years, but by the lifetime of the human spirit. The life of a man is three-score years and ten: a little more, a little less. The life of a nation is the fullness of the measure of its will to live.

There are men who doubt this. There are men who believe that democracy, as a form of Government and a frame of life, is limited or measured by a kind of mystical and artificial fate that, for some unexplained reason, tyranny and slavery have become the surging wave of the future — and that freedom is an ebbing tide.

But we Americans know that this is not true.

Eight years ago, when the life of this Republic seemed frozen by a fatalistic terror, we proved that this is not true. We were in the midst of shock — but we acted. We acted quickly, boldly, decisively.

These later years have been living years — fruitful years for the people of this democracy. For they have brought to us greater security and, I hope, a better understanding that life's ideals are to be measured in other than material things.

Most vital to our present and to our future is this experience of a democracy which successfully survived crisis at home; put away many evil things; built new structures on enduring lines; and, through it all, maintained the fact of its democracy.

For action has been taken within the three-way framework of the *Constitution of the United States*. The coordinate branches of the Government continue freely to function. The *Bill of Rights* remains inviolate. The freedom of elections is wholly maintained. Prophets of the downfall of American democracy have seen their dire predictions come to naught.

Democracy is not dying.

We know it because we have seen it revive and grow.

We know it cannot die — because it is built on the unhampered initiative of individual men and women joined together in a common enterprise — an enterprise undertaken and carried through by the free expression of a free majority.

We know it because democracy alone, of all forms of government, enlists the full force of men's enlightened will.

We know it because democracy alone has constructed an unlimited civilization capable of infinite progress in the improvement of human life.

We know it because, if we look below the surface, we sense it still spreading on every continent — for it is the most humane, the most advanced, and in the end the most unconquerable of all forms of human society.

A nation, like a person, has a body — a body that must be fed and clothed and housed, invigorated and rested, in a manner that measures up to the standards of our time.

A nation, like a person, has a mind — a mind that must be kept informed and alert, that must know itself, that understands the hopes and the needs of its neighbors — all the other nations that live within the narrowing circle of the world.

And a nation, like a person, has something deeper, something more permanent, something larger than the sum of all its parts. It is that something which matters most to its future — which calls forth the most sacred guarding of its present.

It is a thing for which we find it difficult — even impossible — to hit upon a single, simple word.

And yet we all understand what it is — the spirit — the faith of America. It is the product of centuries. It was born in the multitudes of those who came from many lands — some of high degree, but mostly plain people, who sought here, early and late, to find freedom more freely.

The democratic aspiration is no mere recent phase in human history. It is human history. It permeated the ancient life of early peoples. It blazed anew in the middle ages. It was written in *Magna Carta*.

In the Americas its impact has been irresistible. America has been the New World in all tongues, to all peoples, not because this continent was a new-found land, but because all those who came here believed they could create upon this continent a new life — a life that should be new in freedom.

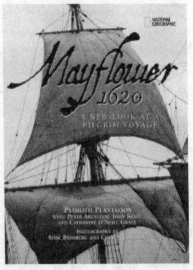

Its vitality was written into our *Mayflower Compact*, into the *Declaration of Independence*, into the *Constitution of the United States*, into the *Gettysburg Address*.

Those who first came here to carry out the longings of their spirit, and the millions who followed, and the stock that sprang from them — all have moved forward constantly and consistently toward an ideal which in itself has gained stature and clarity with each generation.

The hopes of the Republic cannot forever tolerate either undeserved poverty or self-serving wealth.

We know that we still have far to go; that we must more greatly build the security and the opportunity and the knowledge of every citizen, in the measure justified by the resources and the capacity of the land.

But it is not enough to achieve these purposes alone. It is not enough to clothe and feed the body of this Nation, to instruct to inform its mind. For there is also the spirit. And of the three, the greatest is the spirit.

Without the body and the mind, as all men know, the Nation could not live.

But if the spirit of America were killed, even though the Nation's body and mind, constricted in an alien world, lived on, the America we know would have perished.

That spirit — that faith — speaks to us in our daily lives in ways often unnoticed, because they seem so obvious. It speaks to us here in the Capital of the Nation. It speaks to us through the processes of governing in the sovereignties of 48 States. It speaks to us in our counties, in our cities, in our towns, and in our villages. It speaks to us from the other nations of the hemisphere, and from those across the seas — the enslaved, as well as the free. Sometimes we fail to hear or heed these voices of freedom because to us the privilege of our freedom is such an old, old story.

The destiny of America was proclaimed in words of prophecy spoken by our first President in his first inaugural in 1789 — words almost directed, it would seem, to this year of 1941: "The preservation of the sacred fire of liberty and the destiny of the republican model of government are justly considered ... deeply, ... finally, staked on the experiment entrusted to the hands of the American people."

If we lose that sacred fire — if we let it be smothered with doubt and fear — then we shall reject the destiny which Washington strove so valiantly and so triumphantly to establish. The preservation of the spirit and faith of the Nation does, and will, furnish the highest justification for every sacrifice that we may make in the cause of national defense.

In the face of great perils never before encountered, our strong purpose is to protect and to perpetuate the integrity of democracy.

For this we muster the spirit of America, and the faith of America.

We do not retreat. We are not content to stand still. As Americans, we go forward, in the service of our country, by the will of God.

Section A: Text-based Reading Comprehension

I. Choose the best answer according to the passage.

1. What are the real dangers for the Americas now?
   A. Disruption from within
   B. Being in isolation and inaction
   C. Disruption from without
   D. Poverty
2. Which one of the following is true about "democracy" for the Americans?
   A. It is a form of Government and a frame of life.
   B. It is mere recent phase in human history.
   C. It is an ebbing tide.
   D. It is the spirit and the faith of America.
3. Why does Roosevelt say "democracy is not dying"?
   A. Because it is built on the unhampered initiative of individual men and women joined together in a common enterprise.
   B. Because it enlists the full force of men's enlightened will.
   C. Because it has constructed an unlimited civilization capable of infinite progress in the improvement of human life.

D. All of the above.
4. Which one of the following is not the characteristic of a nation for Roosevelt?
   A. It measures up to the standards of our time.
   B. It must keep alert and informed of itself and others.
   C. It can be hit upon by a single and simple word.
   D. It has something deeper and more permanent.
5. What is the main purpose of the address?
   A. To explain the spirit of America
   B. To protect and perpetuate the integrity of democracy
   C. To remind the Americans of the history of democracy
   D. To call for supporting

II. Answer the following questions.
1. What are the main tasks for Roosevelt's administration and his people?

2. What are the perils encountered by the American people?

III. Further discussion.
1. Do some research about the story of *May flower Voyage* and *Mayflower Compact*. What is the significance of Mayflower to the American society?

2. The opening of *The Declaration of Independence*, written by Thomas Jefferson in 1776, states as follows:
   We hold these truths to be self-evident, that all men are created equal, that they are endowed by their Creator with certain unalienable Rights, that among these are Life, Liberty, and the Pursuit of Happiness. That to secure these rights, Governments are instituted among Men, deriving their just powers from the consent of the governed.
   So, how do you understand it?

Section B: Vocabulary

I. Fill in the blanks with the proper forms of the words given below.

disruption	surge	valiant	inviolate	come to naught
ebb	revive	multitude	hamper	invigorate
heed	inaugural	permeate	smother	muster

1. Despite _____ efforts by the finance minister, inflation rose to 36%.
2. She managed to _____ the courage to ask him to the cinema.
3. All their plans _____.
4. Fierce storms have been _____ rescue efforts and there is now little chance of finding more survivors.
5. The smell of roast beef _____ the air.
6. She seemed _____, full of life and energy.
7. The accident on the main road through town is causing widespread _____ for motorists.
8. Snow soon _____ the last of the blooms.
9. She fainted but the brandy soon _____ her.
10. An unexpected _____ in electrical power caused the computer to crash.
11. I was currently divorced and feeling at a very low _____.
12. The change of government _____ a new era of economic prosperity.
13. For centuries the tomb lay _____ until, by chance, it was discovered by two miners.
14. The city has a _____ of problems, from homelessness to drugs and murder.
15. The airline has been criticized for failing to _____ warnings about lack of safety routines.

II. Root and word formation.
A. Study the following roots and list more examples in the space provided.

Root	Meaning	Examples	More examples
-vert (vers)	to turn	avert, adverse, divert	
-vol	will, to fly	volition, volatile	
-volv (volu)	to roll, to turn	evolve, voluble, devolve	
-vuln (vult)	wound	vulnerable, vulture	

B. Fill in the blanks with the proper forms of the words given below.

| devolve | volition | avert | versatile |
| vulnerable | benevolent | revolve | adverse |

1. While he's ill, most of his work will _____ on me.
2. Accidents can be _____ by careful driving.
3. Young men who take steroids can erroneously believe themselves to be _____.
4. The wheels began to _____ slowly.
5. I didn't ask him to go; he went of his own _____.
6. She's a very _____ performer; she can act, sing, dance, and play the piano.
7. We often experience pleasure ourselves upon performing _____ acts.
8. The match has been cancelled due to _____ weather conditions.

Section C: Cloze

Fill in the blanks with the proper forms of the words given below.

| situation | rule | even | comprehend | act |
| man | clothing | but | result | opposite |

Cultures commonly allow a range of ways in which men can be men and women can be women. Culture also tells us how different activities should be conducted, such as how one should __1__ as a husband, wife, parent, child, etc. These rules of permissible behavior are usually flexible to a degree — there are some alternatives rather than hard __2__. In North America, for instance, culture tells us how we should dress based on our gender, but it allows us to dress in different ways in different __3__ in order to communicate varied messages and statuses. The clothing patterns of women in this society can be particularly rich and complex. Their clothing can be intentionally business-like, recreational, as well as sexually attractive, ambiguous, neutral, or __4__ repulsive. North American women are generally more knowledgeable than men about the subtleties of using __5__ and other adornment to communicate their intentions. The wide range of permissible ways of being a woman in North America today makes women somewhat unpredictable as individuals when others are trying to understand their intentions __6__ do not fully comprehend the cultural patterns. It is particularly hard for men from other cultures to __7__ the subtle nuances. This at times can __8__ in awkward or even dangerous situations. For instance, the easy friendliness and casual, somewhat revealing dress of young North American women in the summertime is sometimes interpreted by traditional Latin American and Middle Eastern __9__ as a sexual invitation. What messages do the clothes and body language communicate to you? How do you think they might be interpreted by members of the __10__ gender and by people in other cultures? Do you think that the age of the observer might play a part in their interpretation?

Section D: Reading Skills Training

Directions: The following exercises are meant to improve your fast reading ability. And you are suggested to go over the passages quickly and then answer all the questions within 25 minutes.

Passage 1
    For questions 1 – 7, please mark
    Y (for YES) if the statement agrees with the information given in the passage;
    N (for NO) if the statement contradicts the information given in the passage;
    NG (for NOT GIVEN) if the statement is not given in the passage.
For questions 8 – 10, complete the sentences with the information given in the passage.
1. _____ According to Joan Johnson-Freese, the problem with orbital satellites is that they are easy to be attacked by anti-satellite weapons.
2. _____ The US Air Force has clearly stated the mission of the X – 37B.
3. _____ X – 37B is the only satellite that has passed the Pentagon's hypersonic test.
4. _____ Compared with the US space shuttle, the X – 37B is unmanned and smaller.
5. _____ X – 37 can be used for robotic astronaut.
6. _____ The scientific community all agree that X – 37B is not suitable for mapping imagery.
7. _____ The technology of X – 37B is very similar to the retired shuttle X – 37G.
8. Weeden also suggests the X – 37B's orbit may show that the military is now testing __ _____.
9. According to Gary Payton, the X – 37B is just _____ of the space shuttle type of activities in space.
10. The Air Force's X – 51A Waverider suffered a fatal mishap earlier this year on a test flight and _____.

X – 37B: Secrets of the US Military Spaceplane

In the early morning of 16 June, 2012, a top secret spaceplane made a picture perfect landing at the Vandenberg Air Force Base in California. To those unfamiliar with the vehicle, it might have looked roughly similar to the US space shuttle, the manned spacecraft that shuttled astronauts into space for two decades.

But this spaceplane, called the X-37B Orbital Test Vehicle, is very different. While it looks like a plane, is launched on a rocket, has a cargo bay and uses some of the same technology as the shuttle, such as thermal shielding to protect it during reentry, it is smaller and unmanned. It is designed to stay in orbit for months on end and can automatically land back on Earth. Perhaps more crucially, the Boeing-designed plane is operated by the US Air Force and its mission is a closely held secret, prompting a slew of speculation about its true purpose.

Since the first X-37B was launched in 2010, amateur satellite spotters have carefully followed the robotic spacecraft's orbit, while those unconnected with the program have speculated that the plane could be anything from an anti-satellite weapon to so-called "on demand reconnaissance," shorthand for a spy satellite that can be placed over any country in the world. Compounding the mystery was the launch of a second vehicle in 2011, which stayed in orbit for 469 days, long exceeding the Air Force's stated maximum requirement of 270 days for the spaceplane.

Now, a third launch is slated for 11 December, according to an Air Force spokesperson, once again ramping up the rumour mill. So, what do we actually know about the plane?

Tactical response

Early reports focused on the X-37B's seeming resemblance, at least in size and weight, to the X-20 Dynasoar (short for Dynamic Soarer), a 1950s-era hypersonic vehicle that was envisioned for a variety of military missions, including bombing and sabotaging enemy satellites. However, experts familiar with the X-37B programme emphasized that its technology is actually closer to the recently retired space shuttle (a fact reinforced by Boeings' proposal for a crewed version of the vehicle known as the X-37C). The Air Force blandly described the role of the X-37B in a factsheet given to media as a "reliable, reusable, unmanned space test platform".

The Air Force also says the mini-shuttle has two objectives: testing "reusable spacecraft technologies" and conducting "experiments which can be returned to, and examined, on Earth". Again, this is similar to the stated aims of the space shuttle. But many forget that earlier craft also had a secret military role. Although ostensibly a civilian program, it conducted a series of missions from 1982-1992 on behalf of the National Reconnaissance Office, carrying a series of classified spy satellites.

Similarly, most outside experts now agree that it's likely the robotic space plane is being used for some sort of secret reconnaissance. "I think the guess that makes most sense is quick-response tactical imaging, meaning hours to a couple of days from request to delivery," says Allen Thomson, a former CIA analyst.

Thomson says it is also possible that it could have a more mundane but useful task, such as "maintaining up-to-date general purpose mapping imagery." However, if that is the case, Thomson says that it could be a waste of money. "I think that the commercial satellites could and should do that cheaper and better than X-37B," he says. It is a view backed by parts of the scientific community.

Indeed, the X-37B launches comes in the middle of a larger debate about the role of government-operated spy satellites, which have proven enormously costly but can provide some of the most advanced imagery, versus commercial satellite imagery. The US intelligence community recently slashed its budget for commercial imagery, indicating that it was going back to greater reliance on its own classified satellites.

The view that the X-37B is a reconnaissance platform is strengthened by observations from amateur satellite watchers, who track the vehicles' orbits, and noticed that it has similar orbits to spy satellites and scientific remote sensing craft. In addition, they noticed the craft changing its orbital path several times during its test flights.

This is to be expected, says Joan Johnson-Freese, professor of national security studies at the US Naval War College in Newport. "The upcoming launch will continue just to see what the vehicle can do," she says. "One of the things they are testing is maneuverability. The problem with satellites in orbit is they are very predictably in certain orbits at certain times, and thus vulnerable to anti-satellite weapons (ASAT)."

Johnson-Freese says the military has long been interested in the ability of a spacecraft that has "the ability to evade, to maneuver, to not be in a predicable place at a predicable time."

She expects the Air Force will be "pressing the envelope for manoeuvrability and duration" during the X-37B's next flight. "That will give them the idea of potential missions where avoidance of ASATs comes into play."

"No weapons"

Although its orbits may be difficult to predict in advance, its tracks show where the X-37B has been and its likely purpose, says Brian Weeden, a technical advisor at the Secure World Foundation, a Washington-based foundation that focuses on space issues.

For example, he says, the X-37B flew at inclination of 42.79 degrees, which tells you how far north and south in latitude the spacecraft can see. "The tradeoff is that something at a 90 degree polar orbit covers the whole world, but its frequency is less; it may arrive only every couple of days," he says. "If something is 40 or 45 degrees, it would be covering a smaller portion [of the earth], but more often. "At a 42.79 degree inclination, the X-37B would be useful for looking at a geographic region such as the Middle East, says Weeden, pouring cold water on one theory that that it was used to spy on China's spacelab, Tiangong-1. And given the current political context, he says, the Middle East "makes sense".

Weeden also suggests the X-37B's orbit may indicate that the military is trying out a new sensor system, such as radar imaging or hyperspectral sensors, which collect information across different wavelengths. He suggests this could be the case, because unlike satellites collecting light in the visible wavelength, the X-37B's orbits are not synchronized with the sun, a trick used to maintain a predictable angle between the sun, satellite and ground.

But, like with many of the theories surrounding the X – 37B, he warns, "it is just speculation."

For its part, the Air Force itself is silent about the plane's use, only speaking to allay fears that it was a weapon. "I don't know how this could be called weaponisation of space. It's just an updated version of the space shuttle type of activities in space," said Gary Payton, the Air Force's deputy undersecretary for space programmes, in 2010. "We, the Air Force, have a suite of military missions in space and this new vehicle could potentially help us do those missions better."

Whatever its purpose; the X – 37B is perhaps one of the few bright spots among the Pentagon's hypersonic test vehicle programs. The Air Force's X – 51A Waverider, a scramjet powered hypersonic missile, suffered a fatal mishap earlier this year on a test flight, and never reached hypersonic speeds. Separately, another hypersonic prototype, known as the Falcon Hypersonic Test Vehicle – 2, suffered mishaps in both flight tests, plunging into the ocean.

Those other efforts, which are focused on creating missiles, are still in early testing phase, while the X – 37B is clearly further along.

"I think the one interesting question is whether this is just test and evaluation, or is it being used to be support real world operations," says Weeden. But like most questions about the plane, it is one that is currently impossible to answer.

Passage 2

Like many chapter books, *Shades of Gray* includes several characters, but the protagonist is the principal or central character, ideas, or concept that is the focus of the plot. The central character is presented in greater detail than other characters. The antagonist is a character who is in conflict with the protagonist. The antagonist is sometimes a villain and sometimes a foil character, one whose traits provide a complete contrast to those of the protagonist. An antagonist lends excitement and suspense to a story but is developed with less detail than a protagonist.

The detailed information given about the protagonist usually leads readers to identify with and follow this character throughout the story. In *The Burning Questions of Bingo Brown* by Besty Byars, many readers identify with Bingo's worries about the proper way to hold a girl's hand. His fears and embarrassments as he struggles toward maturity reveal his character, and his unexpectedly antagonistic relationship with his favorite teacher shows the dimensionality of his character, convincing the reader that Bingo will survive his problems.

Bingo Brown is a well-developed protagonist with three-dimensional or round characteristics. Well-rounded characters have complex, multifaceted personalities that readers come to know as they learn about their individual traits, revealed through the trouble in their lives, which never run smoothly. If there were no trouble, there would be no story. Well-rounded characters make readers care and want to know how the characters will resolve their predicaments. Katherine Paterson, in *A Bridge to Terabithia*, acquaints her readers with the character of Jess so well that they can anticipate his actions, reactions, and feelings. They know that he is unhappy in his family and that he has no close friends. They are happy for him when Leslie moves next door and together they create the magic kingdom of Terabithia, where Jess's world changes into a happier place. They mourn with him when Leslie drowns.

All the characters are not developed with the same depth as the protagonist. Supporting characters are flat or less round because they lack the depth and complexity of a real person. These characters are built around a single dominant trait or quality representing a personality type. Flat characters are needed as part of the interactive background; their primary function is to advance the protagonist's development. Fully portraying these characters would make the story too complex for children. Supporting character often include the protagonist's best friend, a teacher, or parents. In *The Village by the Sea*, all of the characters were flat except the protagonist, Emma. Aunt Bea is a flat character whose primary trait is unhappiness caused by alcoholism. Emma's parents are depicted as understanding, but they are flat characters as well.

Some flat characters are stereotypes who lack individualizing characteristics and instead represent traits generally attributed to a social group as a whole. They exhibit a few traits representative of conventional mothers, father, friends, or teachers and are developed quickly with brief bits of information so that drawing their characters does not interrupt the story flow. In traditional literature, all characters are stereotypes representing traits such as good, evil, innocence, and wisdom.

Read the passage above and answer the following questions.

11. According to the passage, the antagonist, a character who is in conflict with the protagonist can sometimes properly be _____.
    A. central character   B. helpless character
    C. negative character   D. unnecessary character
12. Which of the followings is not the characteristic of supporting character?
    A. Lacking the depth and complexity of a real person
    B. Representing a personality type
    C. Advancing the development of protagonist
    D. Changing significantly during the course of a story
13. The main function of flat characters is to _____.

Passage 3

Ethics is a conception of right and wrong behavior, defining for us when our reactions are moral and when they are immoral. Business ethics, on the other hand, is the application of general ethical ideas to business behavior. Ethical business behavior is expected by the public, it facilitates and promotes good to society, improves profitability, fosters business relations and employee productivity, reduces criminal penalties from public authorities and regulators, protects business against unscrupulous employees and competitors, protects employees from harmful actions by their employer, and allows people in business to act consistently with their personal ethical beliefs. Ethical problems occur in business for many reasons, including the selfishness of a few, competitive pressures on profits, the clash of personal values and business goals, and cross-cultural contradictions in global business operations. Ethical issues, such as bribery and corruption, are evident throughout the world, and many national governments and international agencies are actively attempting to minimize such actions through economic sanctions and international codes of ethical behavior. Although laws and ethics are closely related, they are not the same: ethical principles tend to be broader than legal principles. Illegal behavior by business and its employees imposes great costs on business itself and the society at large.

To be precise, business is the art and discipline of applying ethical principle to examine and solve complex moral dilemmas. Business ethics proves that business has been and can be ethical and still make profits. Until the last decade, business ethics was thought of as being a contradiction in terms. But things have changed; today more and more interest is being shown to the application of ethical practices in business dealings and the ethical implications of business. Business ethics is that set of principles or reasons which should govern the conduct of business whether at the individual or collective level.

Ethical solutions to business problems may have more than one right answer or sometimes no right answer at all. Thus logical and ethical reasoning are tested in that particular business situation. A business or company is considered to be ethical only if it tries to reach a <u>trade-off</u> between its economic objective and its social obligations, such as obligations to the society where it exists and operates; to its people for whom it pursues economic goals; to the environment, from where it takes its resources; and the like.

Business ethics is based on the principle of integrity and fairness and concentrates on the benefits to the stakeholders, both internal and external. Stakeholders include those individuals and groups without which the organization does not have an existence. It includes shareholders, creditors, employees, customers, dealers, vendors, government and the society.

Choose the best answer according to the passage.
14. Ethical business problems may happen when _____.
    A. businessmen suffered pressures on profits in competition
    B. there exist conflicts between personal values and business targets
    C. cross-cultural contradictions occur in the international business
    D. All of the above
15. What does the underlined word "trade-off" probably mean in the passage?
    A. A balance achieved between two desirable but incompatible features
    B. An exchange (something) for something else
    C. A settlement of a dispute that is reached by each side
    D. An agreement accepted by two or more opinions, principles, or interests

Further Reading

Struggle for Freedom

Pearl Buck

Stockholm, December 10, 1938

It is not possible for me to express all that I feel of appreciation for what has been said and given to me. I accept, for myself, with the conviction of having received far beyond what I have been able to gibe in my books. I can only hope that the many books which I have yet to write will be in some measure a worthier acknowledgment than I can make tonight. And, indeed, I can accept only in the same spirit in which I think this gift was originally given — that it is a prize not so much for what has been done, as for the future. Whatever I write in the future must, I think, be always benefited and strengthened when I remember this day.

I accept, too, for my country, the United States of America. We are a people still young and we know that we have not yet come to the fullest of our powers. This award, given to an American, strengthens not only one, but the whole body of American writers, who are encouraged and heartened by such generous recognition. And I should like to say, too, that in my country it is important that this award has been given to a woman. You who have already so recognized your own Selma Lagerlof, and have long recognized women in other fields, cannot perhaps wholly understand what it means in many countries that it is a woman who stands here at this moment. But I speak not only for writers and for women, but for all Americans, for we all share in this.

I should not be truly myself if I did not, in my own wholly unofficial way, speak also of the people of China, whose life has for so many years been my life also, whose life, indeed, must always be a part of my life. The minds of my own country and of China, my foster country, are alike in many ways, but above all, alike in our common love of freedom. And today more than ever, this is true, now when China's whole being is engaged in the greatest of all struggles, the struggle for freedom. I have never admired China more than I do now, when I see her uniting as she has never before, against the enemy who threatens her freedom. With this determination for freedom, which is in so profound a sense the essential quality in her nature, I know that she is unconquerable. Freedom — it is today more than ever the most precious human possession. We — Sweden and the United States — we have it still. My country is young — but it greets you with a peculiar fellowship, you whose earth is ancient and free.

I. Read the passage above and decide whether the statement is true (T) or false (F).

1. _____ China and America are very different except their common love for freedom.
2. _____ American writers are quite hopeful of their future recognition.
3. _____ Freedom is the common desire that the people of China has been pursuing.
4. _____ Without freedom, the United States of America is easy to conquer.
5. _____ The Nobel Prize is both for what has been done and also for the future.
6. _____ The United States of America is so young that they are still struggling for freedom.
7. _____ Women writers are well recognized in America.
8. _____ China has exerted equal influence on Pearl Buck's writing.

II. Research and mini-presentation.

Pearl Buck, also known by her Chinese name Sai Zhenzhu, spent most of her life before 1934 in China. Much of her writing was about Chinese culture. Her novel *The Good Earth* was awarded the Nobel Prize in Literature in 1938 "for her rich and truly epic descriptions of peasant life in China and for her biographical masterpieces". Do some researches in the library or on the Internet, trying to find more detailed information about her, and then make a mini-presentation on her contributions to the class.

_____
_____

参考文献

Bressler, C. E. *Literary Criticism*: An introduction to theory and practice. New Jersey: Prentice Hall, 2004.
Brown, D. *The Da Vinci Code*. Anchor, 2009.
Cambridge Advanced Learner's Dictionary. 2nd edition. Cambridge: Cambridge University Press, 2005.
Collins Cobuild Advanced Learner's English Dictionary. 5th edition. Glasgow: Harpers Collins Publishers Ltd, 2008.
Ginsberg, R. The Philosophy of Art. *Idealistic Studies*, 1992, 22 (3): 250-251.
Ingleby, L. C. *Oscar Wilde*: The Philosophy of Beauty. London: T. Werner Laurie, 1907.
Heylighen, F., & Riegler, A. (ed.). *The Evolution of Complexity*. 1999.
Hütter, R. Bound to be Free. *The Christian Century*. 2004, August (10): 24-27.
Longman Dictionary of Contemporary English. 4th edition. London: Pearson Education, 2008.
Sander, S. R. *Hunting for Hope*. Boston: Beacon Press, 1999.
Sontag, S. *Against Interpretation and Other Essays*. Picador, 2001.
William, C. P. Is the Bible True? *The Christian Century*. 1995, October (11): 924-925.
李平武. 英语词根与单词的说文解字. 福州：福建教育出版社, 2008.
牛津高阶英汉双解词典. 牛津：牛津大学出版社, 2008/北京：商务印书馆, 2014.